My Parents Married on a Dare

My Parents Married on a Dare

AND OTHER FAVORITE ESSAYS ON LIFE

CARLFRED BRODERICK

Deseret Book
Salt Lake City, Utah

Library of Congress Cataloging-in-Publication Data

Broderick, Carlfred Bartholomew.
    My parents married on a dare and other favorite essays on life /
by Carlfred Broderick.
        p.   cm.
    Includes index.
    ISBN 1-57345-190-8 (hb)
    1. Marriage—Religious aspects—Mormon Church. 2. Mormon
Church—Doctrines. 3. Church of Jesus Christ of Latter-day Saints—
Doctrines. 4. Broderick, Carlfred Bartholomew. I. Title.
BX8641.B758   1996
230'.93—dc20   96-19270
                                                                CIP

Printed in the United States of America

10   9   8   7   6   5   4   3   2   1

*To my wife, Kathleen, whom I married
after years of sweet anticipation.*

CONTENTS

PART IV:
THE MOST MEANINGFUL ARTICLES
I EVER HAD THE PRIVILEGE OF PRODUCING

PART I:

My Life and Times

CHAPTER ONE

My Parents Married on a Dare

This is the only piece in the collection that was originally written for a professional rather than an LDS audience. Marvin Sussman, himself one of the most creative and productive scholars in the field of family studies and currently editor of *The Journal of Family Issues,* decided to do a special edition of the journal on the personal and professional lives of some of the leading lights in that discipline. I was flattered to be included in this august company and submitted the following account of my own life and times. I apologize to the nonprofessional reader who may find a few paragraphs directed beyond his or her interest, but I am hopeful that for those interested in my life experiences there will be sufficient compensations.

My parents married on a dare. Fred Broderick, an Irish Catholic Brooklynite, had arrived in Salt Lake City by "poor-man's pullman" (i.e., by hopping a freight car) only a few months before. My mother, Napina Bartholomew, had grown up a Mormon in the city of Mormons but was at a vulnerable place in her life. She was living at home and unhappy to be there, and she had a job working in a "mom-and-pop" neighborhood grocery store where "Pop" was, in modern parlance, sexually harassing her. To her, Fred Broderick, ten years her senior, a world traveler, and a veteran of the World War, seemed like a sophisticate. They had been dating off and on for some months when a couple of friends decided on the spur of the moment to run off to Sin City (alias Ogden, the Las Vegas of its day) to get married. They invited Fred and Napina to be the witnesses at their wedding. On the way to Ogden, the eloping couple rode in the front seat of the open coupe, my parents-to-be in the rumble seat. About two-thirds of the way there, the bride-to-be leaned over the backseat and yelled, "I dare you guys to get married too!" And so they did. My mother says of that marriage, that I was the only good thing that came of it.

My entrance into the world a year and a half later was an extended family event. I was born April 7, 1932, in my maternal grandparents' home on Roosevelt Avenue in Salt Lake City. In attendance were a large number of relatives, including, of course, my grandparents, Elizabeth and Carl Bartholomew. Grandmother had been head nurse at the Latter-day Saints Hospital and was an experienced obstetric assistant, but on the occasion of my birth she exercised her Victorian prerogative and fainted.

Grandfather, on the other hand, a hale-fellow-well-met traveling salesman, noted for his practical jokes and inexhaustible store of off-color stories, was calling the color shots. "I can't tell if it's a boy or a girl yet," he yelled over his shoulder to those who couldn't get a close view, "but it's a blond."

In this crowd, my father was the outlander. All of my newborn features were immediately parceled out among the maternal kin: the nose was my grandfather's, the chin was my Aunt Adah's, my ears were a direct legacy from Uncle Jasper. His genetic contributions ignored in the general consensus, Fred Broderick was heard to mumble, "Well, at least he's got my brains." And, perhaps I did.

There was a certain amount of contention over what to name me. The local clan felt that since I was the first grandchild, I should be named Carl Bartholomew

Broderick, after my grandfather. My father was firm in the opinion that I should be named Fred Broderick Jr. A conciliatory aunt finally hit on the compromise, Carlfred (no middle name) Broderick, to which everyone agreed. In the end, however, it was my grandfather who performed the naming ceremony in front of the congregation in the Mormon fashion, and he solemnly pronounced me Carlfred Bartholomew Broderick, "by which name he shall be known throughout his life and on the records of the Church." My parents and a number of others gasped at the perfidy, but the deed was done. My grandmother (whom I suspect of being confederate) commented only, "Well, thank heavens he's not a small child."

My paternal ancestors came to America from County Waterford, Ireland, during the Potato Famine era. My father's grandfather, Richard Broderick, was listed as "twenty years old, occupation carpenter," on the 1851 passenger manifest of the overcrowded *Universe* out of Liverpool. Traveling alone, he was ready to take on the New World. He managed to find work with a contractor in Yonkers—and love. According to family tradition, Ellen Ryan had also recently arrived on these shores in the company of her sister, the last of seven Ryan children sacrificially sent to America by their parents, before they themselves perished from the famine. Richard and Ellen married in 1857. By the time of his death twenty-two years later, of dysentery, he had become proprietor of his own contracting business and was an officer in the local Democratic Party organization. He left his widow with seven surviving children (out of eleven births), all minors. Ellen was a feisty woman who, although illiterate, had a good head for business. For a few months she tried to operate his contracting business by herself, but after it became clear that this was not going to work, she was successful in selling it to a former competitor. She invested the money in tenements and died many years later with an estate substantial enough to cause her surviving children several years of litigation over its distribution.

My father's father, John R. Broderick, was Richard and Ellen's fourth child. He was sixteen at his father's death. At twenty-five he married Susan Murphy, the daughter of another contractor in the area. After trying his hand at several enterprises, he eventually bought and operated the Broderick Bar and Grill on Third Avenue and 39th Street in Brooklyn. My father, the youngest of their eight children, was born in the family apartment over the bar in 1899. Apparently it was not a happy marriage because when Fred was only eighteen months old, his mother abandoned her husband and children for reasons that can only be surmised. The five younger children, including my father, were placed in the Orphanage of the Diocese of Brooklyn. A few months later, their father, John R. Broderick, died of cirrhosis of the liver at age thirty-nine. Two years later, his widow, Susan, also died, leaving the children orphans, indeed.

One by one the Broderick children ran away from the orphanage. The last to leave was my father, the youngest, who finally made his escape when he turned fourteen, as he believed. My own research into the baptismal records of the family prove that he was, in fact, a year older than he thought (and that his "twin" brothers were actually born a year apart). It is poignant evidence of the emotional poverty of the orphanage environment, that these children did not even know their own ages. In any case, he joined the Army in 1914, lying about his age (but by one year less than he thought).

He served in France, driving a munitions truck back and forth to the front. After the War he bounced from job to job and town to town, ending up, as we have noted, at the somewhat unlikely destination of Salt Lake City, Utah.

My Bartholomew ancestors came to Pennsylvania from Germany in the early 1700s, working their way west, generation by generation, through Ohio and Illinois. It is a curious fact that somehow, Carl Bartholomew, my mother's father, managed to find his way to the copper mining community of Bingham Canyon, Utah, and there became the proprietor of a bar and grill. Clearly, if a family coat of arms were ever designed, it ought to feature a bar and grill in the foreground.

It seems to me that my maternal grandparents were an exceedingly unlikely pair. He was a thoroughly worldly man with no religious interests or pretensions, a hard-gambling, hard-drinking, fun-loving man. She was a starchy Mormon nurse working at the local hospital. He was four years younger than she and four inches shorter and roughly the dimensions of Santa Claus. It is reported that she married him to reform him and "because he was the cutest man I ever met." He is said to have married her because she was the only woman he ever met that he couldn't get into bed without marrying her first. Their first child was born in a little apartment over the bar, but by the time my mother was born, Grandma had "prayed him into bankruptcy" to get him out of the tainted business. He went straight and became a traveling salesman. By the time I was born he had also become a Mormon, of sorts, but the kind that drank coffee (and more than once offered to let me taste it, to my grandmother's horror). It was a continuing family embarrassment that he never really gave up having a couple of drinks with his friends from time to time.

Nearly everybody liked my grandfather, but my mother did not, and I think that getting away from home was a part of her motivation to elope with my father. If so, it didn't work. He couldn't keep a job, and they lived with her family for the entire duration of their marriage. She divorced him when I was eighteen months old, and, leaving me with my grandparents, went to California to find a job. On my third birthday, we were reunited in Los Angeles where we came perilously close to starving while trying to live on what she made working in the Sears-Roebuck employee cafeteria. She confesses to having stolen food to feed me, although she would not eat purloined provender herself. When we were finally rescued, she weighed, at 5′4″, only eighty-nine pounds.

Our benefactor was an older second cousin of hers, Allen Howard, whom her mother had sent to check up on her welfare. Within a few months Mom had married him. I give my mother credit: she learned from her marital mistakes (one at a time). Allen Howard was no itinerant ne'er-do-well, but a financially well-established divorcé, who, having taken an early retirement as president of a steel company, had invested in Southern California real estate. To that extent he was a clear improvement over Fred Broderick (who, incidentally, soon after this, disappeared over the horizon, never to be heard from again). From my point of view, however, the new marriage was, at best, a mixed blessing. We did manage to ride out the rest of the Great Depression in comfort and security. But from the beginning, Allen Howard did not like me, and I returned the sentiment. I was never physically abused (thanks to my mother's commitment to the sound principle that "If you don't love him, you can't hit him"), but I remember him, without fondness, as my "wicked stepfather." To the best of my recollection he never permitted a kind word toward me to cross his lips. It was his often expressed view that I was lazy and stupid and worthless and that I badly *needed* the thrashing my mother wouldn't let him administer. (He used to tell the apocryphal story that when my mother took me to kindergarten on the first day she told the teacher, "Carlfred is a very sensitive child; if he does anything wrong, hit the child next to him.")

Fortunately, my mother's alternative view was that I was an extraordinary child, whose destiny was, like cream, to rise to the top in any situation. I dare say that the determination to prove her right and him wrong has been a governing dynamic throughout my life.

He died when I was twelve. I did not mourn his passing; in fact, my unseemly attitude toward his demise so offended one of my schoolteachers that I felt compelled to explain that I had not personally done him in; I just was happy that he was gone.

Mother was married a third time, when I was fourteen, this time to Victor Astley, the mail carrier who had walked our route as long as we had lived there. In my view, he was by far the best of the bunch. For one thing, he had enough sense not to try to parent me, and we managed to work out what began as a pretty good relationship and evolved over the years into a very warm and meaningful one. Vic Astley is the grandfather of my children, and when I use the word *Dad*, I refer to him.

I suppose it must be admitted that I was raised in a "dysfunctional" family, but in truth, I do not think I had any sense of that as I was growing up. Probably part of the reason was that all of my extended kin had families at least as dysfunctional as mine. Just to give a little of the flavor of it, my "Aunt Fern," who lived just across the street and was one of the most present and puissant female relatives in my life, was, to be genealogically precise, my mother's brother's, first wife's, second husband's, father's, 3rd, 4th, and 5th wife. (She married "Uncle Lew" three times in the course of her seven matrimonial ventures.) But beyond lacking a more functional comparison group, I think I was not a particularly introspective or socially insightful child. My interests were in the hard sciences. In the summer between elementary school and junior high, I managed to smuggle myself into a high school physics course and got the highest grade in the class. In high school I was always on the math, physics, and chemistry teams that competed for statewide recognition. In several such competitions I placed among the top ten in the state. On the application form for admittance to Harvard it seemed natural to declare myself a math major. My early conversion to the social sciences was partly a function of the intellectual energy in the Social Relations Department at Harvard in that era. But I wonder if the ground was softened a little by my having had an Aunt Fern.

Before I move on into my academic history, one other aspect of my growing up deserves mention. I grew up Mormon. None of my mother's husbands were believing members of the Church, although long after I left home, Vic Astley eventually joined the Church and even became a Mormon bishop, serving the local congregation I had grown up in. But growing up, one of the axial tensions in the household (I was the other) was the unresolvable conflict between my mother's unwavering, unsophisticated commitment to her faith and Allen Howard's very well-documented and highly sophisticated attacks on all religion. I remember a very early, very conscious decision to aspire to her faith and his scholarship. From an early age I became a student of the scriptures, of comparative religion, and of Church history. And I have never wavered from the faith.

I met Kathleen, the woman I eventually married, at church, when we were both three years old. Our family picture album begins with a picture of our kindergarten class: I was the tallest one in the back row and she was the shortest one in the front. In third grade we were in a play together. I was William Tell, and she was my son. The dramatic scene where William Tell is forced by the wicked Austrians to prove his fabled marksmanship by shooting the apple off his own, beloved son's head was rigged. I was supposed to aim high, and she was supposed to pull on the string attached to the apple. In the event, I knocked the apple cleanly off her head with my first shot. Not too shabby, considering I had never pulled a bow before (nor since). For reasons that escaped both of us, her mother got very upset over the incident and, I think, held it against me all her life.

I had a perpetual crush on Kathleen from kindergarten forward. At fourteen, she was my first date, but in high school we both dated other people, and the first clue I had that she really liked me as more than just her oldest friend was when I got admitted to Harvard and she cried and cried. We married between our junior and senior years in college. By graduation, the first of our eight children was already on the way. Since then, more than forty satisfying years of marriage have come and gone; the children, too, have come and gone, and we are enjoying those much touted (and doubted) pleasures of the empty nest that evaded so many of our contemporaries.

I count it a great good fortune that the years I spent at Harvard (1949–1953) were also part of the golden age of the Social Relations Department there. In a somewhat unusual configuration, it combined sociology, social anthropology, social psychology, and clinical psychology into a single major. George Homans taught the introductory course in sociology, Talcott Parsons taught social structure, Gordon Allport taught social psychology, Clyde Kluckholm, social anthropology, Robert Sears, child development, and Samuel Stouffer and Fred Mosteller taught the two semesters of social statistics. By any measure, that was a star-studded cast.

Of particular importance to me was Carle Zimmerman, who taught the family course. He and his good friend Pitrim Sorokin were out of favor in those years. Their offices were on a different floor from the mainline group, and they were never assigned teaching assistants. Zimmerman remained an associate professor until his retirement, his style of sociology considered passé (partaking of neither the rigorous empiricism of Stouffer nor the grand theorizing of Parsons). It was definitely not politically correct to study with him, but he was the only one teaching about families, so I took his courses anyway (thus establishing a pattern of nonconformity that has served me well ever since).

Carle had let a colleague at the medical school persuade him that a lobotomy would effectively relieve his hypermania with few intellectual side effects. It resulted in slurred speech and a peculiar scrambling of his order of presentation. To compound his problems, I believe he kept a bottle in his desk, and it was easy for colleagues to explain and dismiss him as an alcoholic. But I learned a great deal of good sociology from him. There was an order underlying his presentations, and once I figured out how to decode him, I found his scholarship to be impressive and his ideas exceptionally logical, creative, and thought provoking.

He sponsored my first empirical study. He had developed a theory about the functions of the informal networks of families, and he realized that the temper of the times was such that no one would take his idea seriously without empirical support. Together we developed a questionnaire, and I took it back to Long Beach where, as my undergraduate honors thesis, I collected information on almost 2000 families and their closest friend-families. We published a report on it in *Marriage and Family Living*, the forerunner of the *Journal of Marriage and the Family*, in 1954. It was my first publication. This study, together with those by Marvin Sussman and Elizabeth Bott at the same period, were the first on the nature and function of family networks. In our case, we were interested in network size and homogeneity of the network and how these variables impacted various family issues. We found strong correlations between both variables and the ability of the family to avoid divorce, delinquency, and school dropouts. Somehow in the printing of the article the tables got scrambled so that they could not be readily understood. I have never seen the article cited (except by the authors, of course).

Later, another of Zimmerman's students, Lucius Cervantes, a Jesuit priest, oversaw the replication of the study in eight additional cities, substantiating my findings. When the book reporting this expanded study was published by Zimmerman and Cervantes in 1960, my name appeared only once, in a footnote on page 8, and it was misspelled. As it turned out, it didn't really matter. Zimmerman's chief conclusion from this massive empirical effort was that one should protect one's children from having anything to do with families who were blemished by divorce, delinquency, and school dropouts. Probably there was never a good time for such an idea; certainly it was not in the year John F. Kennedy was elected president of the United States on a platform of social conscience and involvement and outreach. The book was stillborn, an instant antique. The only reason to mourn its demise was the fact that it reported one of the most substantial investigations of family networks, then and since.

Harvard was not all classes and theses, of course. It was a good deal of fun, especially after I was able to bring Kathleen back as my wife. She sang in the Radcliffe Choral Society and I in the Harvard Glee Club. Together we performed some marvelous music with the Boston Symphony under the baton of Charles Muensch: Bach's *B minor Mass,* *St. Matthew's* and *St. John's Passions,* Berlioz' *Requiem,* and Hindemith's *Oedipus Rex.* Also, having an apartment of our own, we became something of the social center of the little community of Mormon undergraduates. We all became very close and have maintained contact over the years. Nearly all of them have gone on to become professionals of substantial reputation—university presidents and the like.

I applied to three graduate schools. Harvard admitted me, but offered no financial support. I had heard of Reuben Hill at North Carolina and of Robin Williams at Cornell, so I applied to both schools and got accepted by both. Cornell offered me $100.00 more, so I went there. In later years, after I got to know Reuben, I sometimes wondered idly what it might have been like to have worked with him and whether my professional interests might have been shaped differently by such an experience.

Cornell was an exciting place also. It turned out that, since my application was to work in the family, I was admitted into the Department of Child Development and Family Relations in the School of Home Economics rather than into the Sociology Department where Robin Williams had his appointment, but I did succeed in getting him as a member of my committee. Urie Bronfenbrenner was there and Harold Feldman, a clinical psychologist of the Rogerian persuasion who had an influence on my later clinical work. Coming to Cornell from Harvard turned out to be a happy circumstance because everyone at Cornell was in awe of the things happening at Harvard. I had just come from the feet of the gods and was viewed as retaining just a bit of the Olympian aura. For example, several faculty members refused to let me sign up for their seminars because they were certain the material would be "old hat" and "derivative." One seminar on Parsons and Bales's new book on the family was canceled after only two or three sessions when it became clear that the instructor didn't understand the somewhat opaque material as well as one of the class members. I confess that this sort of thing did not distress me as much as it might have had I been of a less arrogant disposition. In any case, I plowed right on through the degree in three years, passing the French and German exams on schedule and, if it may be believed, actually enjoying the five-day written and oral qualifying exams. My dissertation followed a class of 100 entering freshmen home-ec majors and predicted the friend-formation process over the first several months, utilizing a similarity/opportunity matrix. It worked out well, although for years I dreamed about that 100 by 100 matrix laid out on our apartment floor. At twenty-four, I had my Ph.D., three children (the third, born the summer after I got the degree), and an exciting new job at the University of Georgia.

Carle Zimmerman had always said that no one ought to be allowed to practice sociology in the United States unless he or she had lived at least four years in the South. I had job offers from BYU and Merrill Palmer; in fact, the job market for Ph.Ds was so favorable in those far-off, palmy days that I actually received telephone calls from the presidents of those institutions. But I chose Georgia because, in addition to my finding Zimmerman's reasoning persuasive, they offered an absolutely top salary and—as a measure of how competitive the bidding for new faculty could get in that era—the rank of associate professor.

In many ways, 1956 was an exciting time to be in that place and situation. *The Brown v. the Board of Education* decision had been handed down by the Supreme Court, and the gears had been set in motion that led to the civil rights movement and eventually reshaped American society. But none of that change had been effected yet. When we got off the plane in Atlanta, we walked into a Quonset-hut air terminal with separate drinking fountains and bathrooms, a cafe open only to whites (no place at all for blacks to get food), and segregated cabs. As a matter of principle we went to the Black and White cab stand. The name sounded progressive. The cabby was very patient with us: "You folk from the North, ain't you? Well, you see the thing is this, I can take you where you want to go, but if I do, won't be no cab for any colored folk. Why don't you folk just take one o' them nice Yellow cabs down there?"

At that time segregation was the fundamental principle upon which all race relations were founded throughout the South. I remember in 1957, the Southeastern Council of the NCFR had its annual meeting in Tallahassee, Florida. We had a handful of black members. There was literally no public facility in Tallahassee that would accommodate us: not a hotel or motel or restaurant, not a civic center, and (most shocking to me) not the University. We finally met in an Episcopal church whose pastor came from New Jersey. It feels as though centuries, rather than decades, have intervened in the social history of the United States since those days.

Everything at Georgia seemed tailor-made for me. I had

this remarkable salary and rank, the established faculty were welcoming (and somewhat in awe of my Ivy League education), and I had a third of my workload freed so I could develop research projects. But as a matter of fact, it was one of the hardest periods of my life. The problems were not in the setting, but in my own expectations for myself. This was my big chance, at last, to do some significant work—under my own name. So I would sit down at my desk, hour after hour, with a set of sharpened pencils and a blank yellow pad, trying to think of something really significant to study. I would covenant with myself that I would know neither food nor water until I had put something *important* on that pad. But in the end I would get nauseous and headachy and come crawling home—where, incidentally, my wife was already fully occupied with three rambunctious, demanding, preschool kids and didn't much need a fourth.

This was the period when I got into therapy as a client. My choice of a therapist was fortunate. She had been one of Carl Rogers's early trainees at Chicago, and in a relatively short time (I think I went for six sessions), I arranged to work through my block and get some research going. The first project (on preschool friendship formation) was a useful learning experience for me, but eventually fizzled. It led me, however, to a second project with a colleague, Stan Fowler, that laid the foundation for the following twelve years of my scholarly life. We got a grant to study the normal sociosexual development of children. At that time the Freudian theory of psychosexual development reigned supreme. But it did not square, either with my own personal experience or with my observation of how actual children developed in their relationship to the opposite sex. In particular, in the aborted study of preschool children's friendship patterns, I had observed, informally, that there was an unmistakable difference in the emotional tone children used in describing same-sex and cross-sex friends. This was not consistent with Freudian doctrine. Moreover, I never experienced Freud's famous latency period. I *always* liked girls and suffered unrequited crushes during that post-oedipal period when I was supposedly oblivious to the whole heterosexual issue. On checking it out with my students, I discovered that my own experience was replicated in most of their memories. So Stan and I decided to challenge the received paradigm and study children in the supposed latency period directly, using a mix of direct questions and projective techniques. The results were dramatic.

Among the fifth and sixth graders we surveyed in that first study, romantic fantasy and heterosexually structured social interaction reigned supreme. Not a whiff of latency anywhere, among about 80 percent of the kids. There was, of course, the often observed segregation of the sexes at the lunch table and elsewhere. But far from being the result of lack of interest in the opposite sex, it grew out of a lack of social skills that made them self-conscious and awkward, effectively preventing their acting on their all too present awareness of the heterosexual potentials of these social situations. But in their fantasies and dreams and even in their conversations with same-sex peers, they exhibited a pervasive attraction to the opposite sex, and the majority explicitly looked forward to dating, courtship, and eventual marriage.

Meanwhile, having found no established congregation of Mormons nearer than Atlanta, seventy miles away, we invited the scattered members of the Church we were able to locate in that area to meet in our home every Sunday. Only a few months after we arrived in Athens, a formal branch of the Church was formed, and I was called to be the first branch president. We soon outgrew our living room, and by the time we left in 1960, we were meeting in a rented hall and had purchased property for our own building. During those same four years, we had two additional children, girls, whom we always referred to as our Georgia belles.

In 1960, when I was twenty-eight years old, I was invited to join the faculty of the College of Home Economics at Pennsylvania State University as a full professor. Fortunately, I had enough sense to insist on coming at the associate level. Although I had never developed a good nose for departmental politics, it did occur to me that a number of associate professors on that faculty would have a good deal more seniority than I, and that some of them just might feel some resentment over such an appointment. It took them nine years to get around to offering me the rank again, but I have never doubted that my decision at that time was the right one (and I can still take private pleasure in knowing that I *could* have been the youngest full professor in the profession if I had been foolish enough to accept the offer).

Based on the work that Stan Fowler and I had done at Georgia, I was able to get a grant from the U.S. Department of Mental Health to expand the research on children's normal sociosexual development. In the end we obtained data from 6000 children from rural, urban, and suburban areas in three states, ages 3–18, plus interview data from a sub-sample of parents. It was a very comprehensive data set with direct questions, projective material, sociometric data, cross-validation from both parents of some of the children—I feel that it is safe to claim that no one else before or since collected as much information on that aspect of children's development.

Since the topic was a "sexy" one, I suddenly found myself getting a lot of media attention. For the most part this was a positive experience. I enjoyed finding my work the subject of articles in all of the news magazines—not to mention *Life, Playboy,* and the *PTA Magazine.* I enjoyed the talk-show interviews.

There are certain risks in this kind of exposure, of course, and early on I stubbed my toe on some of them. For example, in my very first encounter with a major news magazine, at the end of an extensive discussion of my findings, their social implications, and so forth, the reporter thanked me for a good interview, closed his notebook, and asked conversationally how Kathleen and I handled the issue of preteen romantic crushes among our own children. I guilelessly regaled him with a really funny incident that had occurred just that week when my fourth grade daughter had been "dumped" by the boy she loved. It didn't seem such a funny story when it turned up as the final two paragraphs of *Newsweek*'s story on my research. For some time thereafter my name was Mud at my house.

On the other hand, in that same interview I learned about the power of the press in a more positive sense. At one point the reporter had asked me if I considered myself an expert on this subject. Half in jest, since, after all, the subject we were discussing was my own research, I said, "Well, I suppose on this subject I'd have to be considered the world's foremost authority." But even I was taken back at the sheer *hubris* of the headline in the *Newsweek* article: "WORLD'S FOREMOST AUTHORITY ON CHILDREN'S ROMANCES SAYS . . ." Even more surprising was my colleagues' reaction to this claim. Far from being offended, most of them saw that headline and said to themselves (and each other), "By golly, I hadn't realized that Broderick was such an authority." Before that, it had not occurred to me that professionals tend to believe what they read in *Newsweek*, just as others do. That headline did more for my professional reputation than an article in *American Sociological Review*.

I did, of course, publish articles on my findings in professional journals, but I made a mistake in agreeing to publish the comprehensive monograph on the study in a foreign press. Rovalt Verlag of Hamburg, a respected scholarly press, invited me to have the book brought out as one volume in a truly impressive series on human sexuality to which virtually every European and American scholar in the field had committed a volume. Through arrangements with other publishers, the series was to come out not only in German, but also in French, Italian, Dutch, and, of course, English. The German, French, Italian, and Dutch versions came out as promised. Negotiations on the English version broke down, however, and, alas, my first scholarly monograph never came out in the language of the great majority of my professional colleagues.

About that time, I came due for a sabbatical. I applied for a Fulbright Scholarship to go to Ghana to teach for a year at the University of Accra. The application was accepted, and both I and my family were looking forward to a truly enlarging experience in a new cultural setting. (Also, the family was not unmoved by the fact that visiting faculty were treated royally and provided with housemaids and cooks and private swimming pools.) But then we began to see disturbing reports from West Africa. There were anti-colonial uprisings in the interior. One white missionary couple was massacred less than a hundred miles from the university. There were reports of student unrest. Although we were assured that we would be perfectly safe, I simply could not bring myself to put my family at potential risk.

So instead, I applied for a postdoctoral clinical fellowship to be trained as a marriage and family therapist at the University of Minnesota. As it happened, my old friend and mentor, Harold Feldman of Cornell, replaced us in the Fulbright spot. The Feldmans had a life-enhancing, pampered year of tropical stimulation and delight. We got the coldest, longest, dreariest winter in memory in Minnesota. For the family, it was a miserable experience, and I think they never quite forgave me for the switch. A few years later I was recruited as a candidate for Reuben Hill's spot at the University of Minnesota, probably the most prestigious position in the field, at that time, if only because of the stature of the predecessor. When I shared the exciting news of the invitation with my always fully supportive wife, she smiled encouragingly and said, "I think that would be a wonderful opportunity for you, dear, and I want you to know the children and I will write to you every week."

As for me, weather aside, the year in Minnesota had been a stimulating one. I had been doing marriage counseling for a number of years without the benefit of much training or supervision. This was the norm in those days. There was no licensure anywhere and little formal training available. People just worked out their own approaches without anyone telling them what they could or couldn't, should or shouldn't do. But when I became aware of the formal training program at Minnesota with Jerry Neubeck and Dick Hay, I figured I might as well take advantage of it. The hardest part of that year was the return to the lowly status of student. One forgets that the respect freely offered professors in a university community is strictly a function of rank. Students, by contrast, are treated condescendingly by gum-chewing departmental secretaries and are ranked as unemployed bad risks by bank personnel.

The academic part of the program was old stuff for me, but I learned a lot from my clinical internship at the University Hospital and the VA Hospital outpatient clinics, and I became facile at interpreting MMPIs. Most encouraging was the discovery that the clinical style I had already developed survived the scrutiny of my more experienced supervisors.

Coincidentally, that year I was invited to a workshop sponsored by the recently formed Sex Education and Information Council of the United States, better known by its acronym, SIECUS. Mary Calderone had assembled a board of experts to help coordinate and shape the national resurgence of interest in getting better programs of sex education in the public schools. At that time most schools had a menstrual education film for the sixth grade girls, and that was about all. The purpose of this workshop was to put together a resource handbook for the new breed of sex educators. There was really nothing out there for them to draw upon. I was appalled at the stuff they had assembled for us to review for inclusion in this new source book. It was scientifically inaccurate, badly out of date, and heavily burdened with sermonizing. I'm afraid I was characteristically tactless in my outspoken negative opinion of the material and managed to alienate nearly everyone there, including the usually patient chairman, David Mace. I remember leaving the conference feeling that all I had accomplished was to make an fool of myself. "Broderick," I said to myself, "when are you ever going to learn to keep your mouth shut! These people did not really want to hear your opinion. All you managed to do was spit in their soup." No one could have been more surprised than I when a few months later Jessie Bernard, who was head of the SIECUS publication committee, called me and asked if I would be willing to be the editor of this source book. I said, "Can I throw out all the articles you have already collected and start fresh?" She said, "Yes." The result was the first book with my name on it (in English), *The Individual, Sex, and Society,* coedited with Jessie Bernard and published by Johns-Hopkins Press. Putting that book together was a good experience, and the advance they gave me for taking the job saved the family from an otherwise enveloping poverty that had resulted from trying to maintain two residences and live on a sabbatical income.

We returned to Penn State for three more years that turned out to be productive ones for me. In addition to continuing to publish research papers, I was invited to succeed Marvin Sussman as the editor of the *Journal of Marriage and the Family.* That was an exciting time to be editor of the most prestigious journal in the family field. Family scholarship was exploding in every direction during the late '60s. After a year of trying to keep up with all of the new developments, it occurred to me that it would probably be helpful to publish a review of the decade's achievements. The result was the first *Decade Review* in 1970, which, it pleases me to note, was imitated by later editors and so became only the first in a series of decade reviews in the *Journal*. Another innovation that I believe was a step forward was the establishment of an international section and editor. U.S. family scholars tended to be altogether too insular, and this was intended as a partial corrective.

By all odds my most hair-raising (actually hair-graying) experience as editor of the *Journal* grew out of a decision to sponsor an issue featuring the new, and at that time somewhat militant and raw, feminist family scholarship. It was a well-intended effort to expose our readers to a challenging new approach to the analysis of matters familial, and I suppose it constituted a watershed event in the history of the field, but as a personal experience it was simply horrific. I commissioned a distinguished feminist scholar to edit the special edition, gave her the page constraints, a number of copies of the JMF author's style guidelines, and a firm deadline for the edited manuscripts to be in my hands for final copyediting.

She didn't come within a month of meeting any of the deadlines, and she commissioned twice as many papers as I had authorized. The bibliographic references at the end of each article were unfinished or absent, the manuscripts were single-spaced, frequently written on both sides of the paper, and coffee-stained. They were peppered with four-letter words and—even worse, from an editor's perspective—poor grammar and sentence structure. About three-fourths of the pieces had no scholarship to them; they were just hate pieces against men and the patriarchal establishment. The remaining one-fourth I thought had some merit, although even those needed an extraordinary amount of editorial work to put them in shape for publication. I told her which ones I would agree to publish; she told me that I would publish them all, or she would pull them all. Mind you, we were already running two months late on getting out this quarterly issue and in jeopardy of losing our second-class status with the post office if we delayed much longer. It was an editor's worst nightmare—these women were not into compromise for the good of all. As far as they were concerned, the *Journal* (as surrogate for patriarchal society) owed women for thousands of years of injustice. From my point of view, it was blackmail, pure and simple.

In the end, I absolutely refused to publish a few of the articles and insisted on strongly editing some of the others to try to bring them into some approximation of acceptable journal style, but we finally had to give up two entire issues of the *Journal* to accommodate all of the pages of manuscript that were left. When the issues finally reached *Journal* readers they were not charmed by the unaccountable dedication of so many pages to material of such uneven quality. Reuben Hill, for one, charged me with "selling out" to the feminists.

In retrospect, I still think it was a good idea to expose our traditional readership to the winds of feminist critique that were beginning to make themselves felt in the early '70s and that have since truly reshaped the field of family scholarship. But the experience literally turned my hair white. I try to think of my snowy crown as a marker on the path of gender liberation.

At Penn State I maintained my active participation in Mormon affairs and eventually ended up presiding over the Central Pennsylvania District of the Church. I was also more active than ever, before or since, in campus politics. At various points I chaired the Graduate Faculty of the University and the Academic Standards Committee of the University Senate. This was the late '60s and early '70s and, like other campuses, we had to face a student revolt. Students occupied buildings and tried to burn down the ROTC Building. I remember sitting up all night in one of the entrances to our college office building to try to discourage students from setting it to the torch. Other faculty sat in other doorways. We were not armed; we didn't even have any way of communicating with each other, but we believed that the students would not want to hurt anyone, just to make a statement about the establishment. It was a scary night, but nobody came to torch our building (although there were fires set elsewhere). The university president fared less well. A mob of students took an ax to his front door, and, while he and his wife and eighty-year-old mother fled out the back door, entered and ransacked the house. The next day we had a full complement of state militia, armed, in white helmets and spats, guarding the campus. It was just after the Kent State tragedy in very similar circumstances, but we were lucky and no one got hurt.

Those were interesting days on many campuses. I remember the day the students shouted down the Faculty Senate and grabbed the microphone from the president. Some of the younger faculty were very sympathetic to their cause and style of pursuing it. It was necessary to disband the Senate for a period of months. The spirit of the times pervaded the classroom also. I remember one graduate seminar in which I asked the students to assume that the student revolt had fully triumphed, the establishment was overthrown, and local student soviets ruled supreme. What, if any, of the old society's norms would be worthy of preservation? After some heated debate they agreed that there would be no laws against murder or rape because in order to support such laws you would have to reinstitute the whole hated apparatus of society: police, jails, judges, governments— better to suffer a few murders and rapes. The depth of their commitment to ecological values and to the zero-population dogma was such that they would have defined only one act as a capital offense: having more than two children. The revolutionary passions and certitudes of those days are difficult to credit in these more laid-back times, but they were fiercely real then.

In 1970 I got an offer to come to the University of

Southern California to head up their Ph.D. marriage and family therapy program. It was housed in the Department of Sociology, a real anomaly then and now, but that's where James Peterson had his academic appointment when he started the pioneering program in the early 1950s. When Jim moved over to help establish a new School of Gerontology in 1969, the department had to decide if they wanted to keep this clinical option as part of their offering. There were arguments on both sides, but persuasive on the plus side was the fact that, then and now, some of the best students who applied to the department were attracted by the opportunity to be trained as a marriage and family therapist while earning a respectable Ph.D. in sociology. So they decided that if they could find a bona fide sociologist who also was qualified to train clinicians, they would retain the program. In the interview, it appears that I was able to persuade them that my somewhat marginal credentials as a sociologist, or, for that matter, as a clinical trainer, were sufficient for the purpose. Perhaps it helped that I brought the *Journal of Marriage and the Family* with me. In any case, in the fall of 1971, I returned to the area where I had grown up, where all of my relatives still lived, as professor of sociology and executive director of the Ph.D. program in Marriage and Family Therapy at the University of Southern California.

It had not been an easy decision to leave Penn State. It would not be overstating the case to say I had it made there. I had tenure, quality colleagues, and an ongoing Ph.D. program in family relationships, which attracted excellent students and was regarded as one of the strongest in the business. Moreover, at that point in my career I was heavily involved in campus politics (for example, being a member of the President's "Kitchen Cabinet," a circle of informal advisors that had a great deal of influence on what went on at the university). State College, Pennsylvania, was a beautiful place to live and raise a family. Taking it all together, I asked myself, why would I want to move? Then it hit me. At thirty-nine years of age, I was already feeling seduced by the siren song of a serene and certain future. That settled the question; I had better move on to new challenges before hardening of the arteries set in. And besides, the children could get to know their grandparents and cousins.

The new position was a challenge. I don't suppose I had ever before in my life felt a greater need to master an unfamiliar literature in a shorter time, so as to bring myself "up to speed" as both a sociologist and a clinical trainer. Because, to be perfectly honest, although I knew a great deal about the family and about human sexuality, there were oceans of pertinent information that a competent, all-purpose sociologist might be expected to know that were not within my scope of expertise. I had a great deal of clinical material to cover, as well, before I could feel comfortable as a graduate mentor to these students. It would be only a slight exaggeration to say that the move forced me to take a second, informal graduate degree in the areas of my deficits. I liked that.

At USC I managed to keep out of local campus politics but got involved, instead, in the politics of the profession. Once my term as editor of the *Journal* was finished, I managed to find myself elected first, President of the Southern California Association of Marriage and Family Counselors (1974), then President of the National Council on Family Relations (1976), and finally, President of the Association of Mormon Counselors and Psychotherapists (1982).

I took particular pleasure in serving as President of NCFR because that organization had always been, and remains, my professional home base. Most of the people who have been important in my professional life are regularly attending members. I think I have missed only one annual meeting (1975—I had the flu) since 1960. There is not much that one can do of lasting significance in a one-year term of office, but I think fondly of three accomplishments of that

year. First, I was able to persuade the organization to sponsor the first few years of operation of the *Journal of Family
History* under the editorship of Tamara Hereven. To that
small extent, I felt a sponsor of the then new and now thriv-
ing subdiscipline of family history. Second, I represented
NCFR and American family scholars in helping the
Australian Family Life Movement, under John Robison's
leadership, celebrate their fiftieth anniversary. And third, I
held the very first nonalcoholic president's reception. The
event turned out to be a big success, but up to the last hour
there were rumblings that the traditionalists and heavy
drinkers would either boycott it or usurp it, bringing their
own liquor to spike the punch. With the money we saved
on drinks we were able to afford a very nice buffet indeed.

The '70s marked something of an intellectual watershed
for me. Prior to that period, most of my scholarly work had
centered on children's sociosexual development. I had
always been interested in family theory, but until I assigned
myself the task of reviewing the family theory literature of
the 1960s for the decade review, I had never done any serious writing in this area. I believe I am correct in stating that
my 1971 article, "Beyond the Five Conceptual Frameworks:
A Decade of Development in Family Theory," was the first
to bring the new family systems approach to the attention
of mainline family scholars. Prior to that it had pretty much
been confined to family therapists. Later that year Reuben
Hill came out with a paper on family systems theory, com-
paring it to his own developmental approach, but it was
published in a Belgian journal and not many American
scholars saw it. Toward the end of the decade, I was one of
the participants in the major theory construction project
headed by Wesley Burr, Reuben Hill, Ivan Nye, and Ira
Reiss, which eventuated in the two-volume handbook
Contemporary Theories about the Family. I had a chapter,
coauthored with a graduate student, in the first volume
that attempted to summarize the family process theory of

socialization. For Volume II, Jim Smith and I tried the more challenging job of attempting to present a digest of the general systems approach to family processes. Subsequently I have attempted to follow up on those initial efforts with an article on family process theory in Jetsey Sprey's 1992 book *Fashioning Family Theory* and finally with a book-length treatment of the subject, *Understanding Family Process: The Basics of Family Systems Theory* (Sage, 1993).

Besides theory, my interest turned more and more toward the clinical (*The Therapeutic Triangle*, Sage, 1983) and toward the history, both of the clinical branch of family scholarship ("The History of Professional Marriage and Family Therapy," with Schrader, in Gurman & Kniskern, 1984, 1991) and the nonclinical branch ("To Arrive where We Started: The Field of Family Studies in the 1930s," JMF, 1988). I also did a reasonably successful trade book (*Couples*, Simon & Schuster, 1979, and still in print) and a college text, *Marriage and the Family*, now in its 4th edition.

I've continued as an active Mormon, serving as a bishop and as a stake president (the next higher administrative level over bishops), and I even wrote a book on marriage for the Mormon audience, *One Flesh, One Heart* (Deseret Book, 1986).

As one of the more senior statesmen in the field, I get invited to do a fair number of workshops and keynote addresses and perspective pieces and chapters in other people's books. I even get invited to do commencement addresses, from time to time, surely one of the stiffest challenges for any speaker. I still head up the Marriage and Family Therapy Program in the Department of Sociology at USC.

As one with deep roots in the field, I am easily seduced into projecting my own view of its future (although, as a social historian I am painfully aware of how misaimed most future telling turns out to be). Perhaps the most prevalent contemporary view is that the future belongs to the feminist and conflict theorists and to the postmodern constructivists. As my publications document, I am betting that the most profitable direction for future research and theory lies in the investigation of what Hess and Handel, years ago, called the psychosocial interior of the family. The immediate challenge is to discover the metarules governing the patterning of family processes through the careful observation of families in real time (that is, over the course of seconds, minutes, and hours, rather than merely in developmental time or in cross-sectional stop-time). In my view that is the frontier that beckons. The effort to understand how families operate in real time started with the observations of family therapists, and I trust that this group of professional family observers and manipulators will continue to make important discoveries. But the future belongs to the new breed of well-tooled, eclectic, hard-headed, family research scholars. They will discover still better ways to probe the interior of families and to take advantage of the enormous laboratory provided by the variety of family forms and the high rate of family formation, dissolution, and reformation that is prevalent in this historic period. I see a generation of them just emerging from graduate school, and, as all commencement speakers, everywhere, I am encouraged that the future of the field is in good hands.

CHAPTER TWO

The Core of My Faith

I conceive of this piece as the complement to the first chapter. It explicitly tracks my spiritual odyssey as I moved through the career path outlined there. Necessarily there is some overlap, and I apologize in advance for telling a few of my favorite growing-up stories a second time, but I figure any faithful Latter-day Saint must have developed a substantial tolerance for repetition.

A few years ago, Philip Barlow was director of the LDS Institute of Religion at Cambridge, Massachusetts, home of Harvard and Radcliffe and MIT and a fair number of other well-established institutes of higher learning, and was working toward his Ph.D. in religion at Harvard. It was a natural setting for stirring up the inspiration to ask a group of faithful LDS scholars in various fields how they had managed to resolve the built-in tensions and challenges between the skeptical world of secular scholarship and the life of faith. The resulting collection was published as a book, Philip Barlow, ed., *A Thoughtful Faith: Essays on Belief by Mormon Scholars* (Centerville, Utah: Cannon Press, 1986). It contained twenty-two essays, the great majority of which, to my mind, were rather wonderfully inspiring. I was amused to discover that the first press we considered publishing with thought that some of the material in my essay might be "offensive" to refined LDS readers. For this and other reasons, Barlow went with a less protective publisher. What is provided here is the unexpurgated version of my essay. With that build-up, I fear that the reader looking for something provocative will be disappointed. On the other hand, if it is simply that I have, like so many therapists and social

31

scientists before me, become jaded to the canons of spiritually refined writing, you are encouraged to close your eyes to the offensive parts.

M any a night as I grew up, I lay awake listening to my mother and stepfather argue in their bedroom, which was separated from mine only by a thin wall. As I remember, two topics were the major themes of their sometimes heated discussions. One was me. It was my stepfather's passionate belief that I was stupid, lazy, ill-disciplined, and would "never amount to anything." My mother's more serenely held view was that I was like cream and would rise to the top in any situation by virtue of my natural superiority. I suppose it is not overstating the case to say that I have spent most of my life attempting to prove him wrong and her right.

The other topic of contention was religion. It would be hard to imagine two less evenly matched debaters on the subject. He was a gospel scholar of the first rank who could, literally, tell you the content of any chapter in the Standard Works without looking it up. My mother, as he used to say, was not certain whether Second Nephi was in the Old Testament or the New. But though he was remarkably knowledgeable about the gospel, he believed none of it. Mother said he lost his testimony on his mission where he was appointed the personal secretary to the president the day he arrived and for three years spent his full time dealing with troubled and rebellious elders or Church politics. In all that time he never knocked on a door or bore his testimony, but he did study.

In their standard argument he would point out to my mother (*forte*) the contradictions in some series of scriptures (such as the various accounts of the resurrection or the conflicting revelations on the foundation of Zion in Missouri or Zion's Camp or the United Order or polygamy).

Her response (*piano*) was always that she didn't know much about this particular issue but she did know this . . . , and then she would bear her testimony to him and he would, likely as not, put his fist through a wall or door out of sheer frustration.

Early in my life I decided which side of that argument I was on. But I think I also must have decided that I wanted to match his scholarship with her faith. He died when I was twelve, and I inherited his extensive Church library. By the time I was fourteen I had devoured all of it, including his well-marked Standard Works. Not that I waited for him to die to begin reading scriptures or Church books. I remember once at age eleven being reprimanded by my mother for missing the afternoon session of stake conference because I was engrossed in a new book on Book of Mormon geography that was in the seventies' book display in the foyer.

It goes without saying that all of that religious precocity made me an obnoxious child, the bane of every Sunday School teacher. Once when I was ten, I was sent home for explaining to the class what "Thou shalt not commit adultery" really meant. It had seemed clear to me from her explanation that our teacher did not quite understand the concept. Indeed, Sunday School would have been totally insufferable to me if it had not been for one other smart kid in the class, Kathleen. My habit was to attack the teacher's point (whatever it might be) and Kathleen's was to defend it. Since we were evenly matched, this added some life to the otherwise tedious and repetitious material. I eventually married her (i.e., Kathleen), having become addicted to the intellectual stimulation that her independent intelligence added to my life.

From the beginning, I suppose, my life experience predisposed me to segregate matters of *faith,* which were based on personal experience with the Spirit (my mother being the model), and matters of *doctrine,* which were subject to derivation, documentation, and debate. I read every work

Joseph Fielding Smith (and later, Bruce R. McConkie) ever published and honored them as among the greatest scriptorians and doctrinal expositors of the Church. Yet I was always aware of some of the alternative views of Elders Talmage and Widtsoe and President McKay. I remember as a teenager that Kathleen and I approached President McKay (who had come to dedicate the new stake center) and asked him to resolve an issue concerning evolution that we had been discussing. He looked at us and said, "The thing you need to remember about evolution is that the Lord has never revealed anything about the matter. People have their opinions, but the Lord has not revealed the details of how he created the earth."

At a less sublime level I remember the time our bishop came to talk to the priests quorum on "self abuse." This was a man whom I looked up to as a spiritual giant, who could bring tears to my eyes with his testimony. Yet I heard him explain on this occasion (with the same fervency of conviction that he evinced when bearing witness of more sacred things) that we ought not to abuse ourselves because the practice would weaken our minds—that if we spent all of our life fluids as young men we would have nothing left when we needed it later in life. I don't suppose that there was a priest in the room who believed a word of this. The disturbing thing, to me at least, was that he did not differentiate between what he knew by the Spirit and what he believed from folklore. I was grateful that my testimony was independently derived and not dependent upon his credibility as a witness. And I think I vowed to myself never to repeat his error, that is, always to differentiate the core of my faith from the extended corpus of my beliefs.

One last experience in my late teens might perhaps be cited as contributing to my differentiation between spiritual leadership and doctrinal sophistication. As a seventeen-year-old freshman at Harvard, I had the great privilege of getting to know my first General Authority on other than a conference-visitor basis. Elder S. Dilworth Young , one of the Presidents of the Seventy, was the mission president and would invite students over to his home for firesides once a month. I was delighted at the opportunity to get an informed opinion on many of the doctrinal imponderables that I and the little clutch of faithful LDS Harvard students debated in our weekly Sunday afternoon discussions. For starters, one evening I cornered him and asked how he had resolved the paradoxical issues around the nature of our spiritual birth as described in the early chapters of the Book of Moses. It took several minutes of confusing noncommunication before it dawned on me that this great man not only did not have an informed opinion on the matter, but he scarcely understood the issue and frankly had concerned himself very little with such obscure doctrinal points. Once more I had confirmed the lesson of my childhood—that spiritual maturity and inspirational power (which this man unquestionably had in abundance) need not be packaged together with advanced intellectual questing.

Meanwhile, my own experiences led me to pursue each half of the equation. Harvard (and later, Cornell, where I got my Ph.D.) were wonderfully challenging environments. I scarcely read a textbook in my whole educational career— always I was sent to the original source, even if it was in a different language. (I remember having to learn enough Portuguese to get through the reading assignment for a course on world exploration in the sixteenth century.) At the same time, I was constantly being given levels of ecclesiastical responsibility beyond my age or experience because I was living in the mission field. The Church's system of lay leadership has always struck me as one of the most ingenious mechanisms of socialization ever invented. I am puzzled that social analysts and commentators take so little note of it. It is sheer genius to take the very groups that in the ordinary nature of things are most likely to challenge authority and orthodoxy and put them *in* authority and *in charge* of orthodoxy. So they call nineteen-year-old males (surely the most ungovernable and intellectually rebellious group imaginable) to convert the world to believe our doctrine and follow our authorities. Similarly they choose the educated, active, competent, and critical man or woman to head up Church units and serve as the very agents of orthodoxy. I was not called on a mission, mostly because the nation was involved in the Korean War at the time and Truman had slapped a quota on the Church of one missionary per ward (being of the opinion that missionaries were merely draft-dodgers in dark suits). The other part of the reason was that at the tender age of twenty I married Kathleen and took her back to share my senior year at Harvard with me.

But if I missed the experience of a full-time mission, I was fully engaged in various leadership opportunities. In Cambridge Branch I served as Aaronic Priesthood general secretary (roughly equivalent to the Young Men president today) and in the elders quorum presidency. At Cornell I once served in five callings simultaneously: I served as Young Men president at the mission, district, and branch level; as high councilor in the district; and as elders quorum instructor. When I took my first job at the University of Georgia, Kathleen and I founded the branch and I became its first branch president. Later, when we moved to Penn State, I served in the district high council, on the mission board in various capacities, and finally as district president. When we moved to California, I eventually became a stake president. From all of these opportunities has come a rooted certainty that the work is true. The evidence is experiential and overwhelming in its depth and breadth. I have never been permitted the luxury of being a dabbler in the gospel or in the Kingdom. At every point I have been up to my elbows in prayerful application of gospel principles to the real challenges of individual lives and of the humanly textured Church organization.

As district president in State College, Pennsylvania, I was frequently confronted with Ph.D. candidates who informed me that they felt their calling was to complete their degree and that they intended to abstain from all other Church callings until they had finished. I invariably reminded them that the keys for making calls resided not in them but in their branch and district and mission presidents. Not one (of several dozen) ever escaped being given substantial opportunities to serve, and not one went sour from over-extension of their intellectual development while their spiritual selves atrophied. I believe this is the key to the resolution of intellectual and spiritual tensions: full-throttle involvement with both.

That is not to say that I have never experienced serious conflict between these two components in my life. My research efforts in the early 1960s were centered on tracing the development of normal heterosexual development among children and adolescents. In fact my first book was entitled *The Individual, Sex, and Society* and my second (which was translated into German, Dutch, French, and Italian) was titled *Sexual Development in Childhood and Youth*. The publication of these materials, plus research articles that appeared in professional journals, placed me in the fore-front of research in this area for a time, and in addition to receiving a great deal of media attention, I was frequently invited as a consultant to school systems, which were begin-ning to awaken to their responsibility to provide informa-tion and guidance to their students in this area. I traveled all over the world in this capacity during the late '60s and eventually was invited to be a member of the Sex Information and Education Council of the United States (SIECUS), which was the informal resource center for the whole burgeoning sex education movement of that decade. I was honored to take my place among such distinguished colleagues as John Money, David Mace, Ira Reiss, Harold Christiansen, William Masters, Wardel Pomeroy, and Mary

Calderone, to mention only a few of the great scholars who constituted that blue ribbon board. Moreover, I felt that the movement could use an LDS perspective to balance some of the more radical views held by some of its members. The board came under a great deal of attack from the far right, but I knew from my own involvement with SIECUS that their charges of communist allegiance and corrupted morals were baseless and irresponsible. Even when a little filmstrip put out by the John Birch Society entitled "The Rape of Innocence" singled out me and two other board members as "comrades" with red hammers and sickles superimposed on our photos and referred to us as the corrupters of youth, I was more flattered than perturbed. I knew I was no such thing and that the entire purpose of the sex education movement was to inform children about their own bodies and about the realities of the sociosexual world, which information could not corrupt them. Ignorance can corrupt, not information. Besides, I flattered myself that I was at that time anxiously engaged in good works and bringing to pass much righteousness as president of the Central Pennsylvania District of the Pennsylvania Mission, which stretched across the entire rural diagonal of the state, at various times including branches as remote as Scranton-Wilkes-Barre in the northeast and Uniontown in the southwest corner of the state. Every Sunday I was on the road in all types of weather, shoring up the Saints and helping to sustain the struggling branches throughout the area. The work was gratifying, the people were responsive, even the statistics looked good (compared to other districts of similar makeup). I knew I was guided by the Lord in my ministry, and I felt comfortable with the virtue of my work in the sex education movement, too.

As a result I was totally unprepared for what happened . . . well, no, that is not true. The Lord had actually prepared me in a fashion that I did not appreciate until later. I had received a letter from a professional colleague whom I had known for years and who, like myself, was involved in Church leadership positions and in what he used to refer to as the "forefront of the explosion of information and understanding of man's sexual nature." His interests were different from mine and, in my view, more fringy. Among other things, he had become involved in research into nudist groups and had eventually come to feel that the innocent frankness of the sunshine set was wholesome and ought to be emulated. Apparently he had discussed his activities and enthusiasms with his own stake president, who had taken a sophisticated, permissive posture on the matter. But eventually my colleague wrote a paper on his work that attracted general media attention and prompted a letter from a General Authority who suggested that the roles of priesthood leader and nudist advocate were incompatible and that he would have to choose which he wanted to be.

He was mortally offended and intellectually outraged. He was confident that the Brethren were reflecting their "Wasatch-Front" culture and not the will of the Lord, who, he pointed out, had created us naked. But he was also shaken to be put in jeopardy of losing his capacity to serve in the Church. He wrote me an agonizing letter asking for my counsel, feeling that I might be someone who could understand his plight.

I took the responsibility of replying very seriously. I began by acknowledging that it was cheap to give advice from the outside of a situation but that I had tried to put myself in his place, supposing that, for example, the Brethren had come out against sex education, which I was passionately committed to. Then I told him that I had searched my soul as deeply as I could as to how I would respond in that situation and that I could come up with only two possibilities: either 1) I would conclude that the Brethren were exercising their appointed duty to keep watch over the Church and were legitimately calling me back from a path I had wandered into that could lead me away from the goal that we all share, or 2) I would conclude that the Brethren were reacting to my work from a position of differing cultural and generational background, rather than revelation; but in that case I would consider it my duty to make the Abrahamic sacrifice and sustain them anyway, as I have, after all, covenanted to do. I could not, for myself, entertain any third alternative.

Three weeks later my family and I were watching general conference on television, and we heard President Alvin R. Dyer of the First Presidency describe SIECUS (by then, I was a member of the five-person executive committee) as an organization led by evil and conspiring men who were seeking to lead the youth of our nation astray. I felt as though I had been cleaved asunder by an ax. There were only three men on the executive committee, and two of us were Mormons. My oldest daughter got up and stomped out of the room, declaring that she didn't listen to conference to hear her father slandered. Once I recovered enough to begin to think clearly, I decided that what had surely happened was that some of the scurrilous anti-sex education material put out by the far right had been given to the Brethren. Taken at face value, it would alarm anyone. What I needed to do was write for an appointment with President Dyer to put the record straight. But before I wrote to Church headquarters, I went to my office at the university and pulled out my correspondence file to reread the letter I had written to my friend. As events transpired, he chose not to follow my counsel, but I did. I fully believe the Lord provided that opportunity for me to be able to formulate my response in a nondefensive mood so that when I needed it, I was certain what I must do.

President Dyer did agree to meet with me and the other Mormon on the SIECUS executive committee. To my surprise he brought with him a staff (for some reason it had escaped my awareness that General Authorities had staffs) who in turn brought a traveling file drawer with every article

I and the other brother and the rest of the SIECUS Board had ever written—all content analyzed. Actually they did not criticize my own writing, but they did find in general that the SIECUS position was value-free and that that was exactly the opposite of the gospel position. My colleague tried to defend this as the position required of all scientists and scholars, but President Dyer kept coming back to the point that it was contrary to the gospel position to treat these matters in a value-neutral way.

The bottom line was that it would please the Brethren if we let our association with SIECUS lapse, lest we lend our reputations to a movement that ran counter to the Plan. In all honesty, my nonrenewable term was about up, so it was little sacrifice to agree to follow their counsel (it was not coercive; there were no threats). I did ask what I should do about the address urging parents to take a more active role in the sex education of their children, which I had contracted to give in New York at the American Medical Association meetings and also in San Francisco at the National School Board Association meeting that June. President Dyer suggested I submit the talk to President McKay. I did and received back a letter approving the talk "provided it was delivered with the proper spirit."

That may be the only talk on behalf of sex education ever approved by a prophet. It is also the only time in my life I gave a speech with no jokes or ad-libs, exactly as it was written.

But a hard thing happened just a week or two after my meeting with President Dyer and his staff. Someone confided to me that he had overheard a visiting General Authority tell the mission president that if he were in the president's place, he wouldn't leave a man like me in a position of authority for five minutes. The following Sunday the mission president made an unscheduled visit to our district and released me. He had a hard time explaining why he was doing it, so I helped him out: "Nothing personal, just to give various brethren a chance to serve, right?" "Oh yes! That's it!" he replied gratefully.

I was wounded. I felt I had taken counsel and done everything I had been asked to do; in fact, no one had ever accused me of doing anything wrong, yet I felt I was being punished. I loved the people of my district, and I loved the particular claim on the Spirit of the Lord that is incident to such a calling. I had plans and projects and commitments that would now fall to another to implement or ignore. For a year following that, my only calling was as a home teacher.

I will say on my own behalf that I did not withdraw from Church or from my personal prayers. I never spoke a word of complaint to anyone, including my wife and children. I do not remember taxing the Lord with the unfairness of it all, but in my heart I felt that I had been tried out of court and blackballed. At thirty-eight, I felt that my years of service to the Church had been unfairly, prematurely, and permanently ended.

Soon afterward I got a job offer from the University of Southern California. It was an exciting opportunity, and all of our relatives were in California, but I would never have left the Central Penn District if I had not been previously released from my responsibilities to it.

Our new stake president was a contractor and had never heard of me or of SIECUS. He came to like me, and within a few months of our arrival, I was the stake Sunday School president and then stake Young Men president. After about a year they split our ward. As always happens when the news of such a plan is announced, there was speculation about who the new leadership would be. I had myself participated in the process of dividing Church units and felt I knew how it worked. As it happened, on our side of the line there were a couple of older brethren who had been bishops twenty years before and a whole rash of young couples in their late twenties with small children—but in the middle, in their thirties and forties, the bracket from which bishops are usually chosen, there was an echoing emptiness—except for me. Frankly, if I had been the stake president, I would have chosen me as bishop. Nor did this possibility escape the notice of others. People started calling me "Bishop" and watched my response to get a clue if they were right. At least one such was the wife of a high councilor. I figured she might know. I got a haircut and waited for the call. It never came. The twenty-seven-year-old elders quorum president was sustained.

The scenario was plain to me. The stake president had nominated me, the high council had approved the nomination (leaked it to their wives), and sent it on to Salt Lake City—where it had been disapproved on the grounds of my work with SIECUS. I smiled grimly at the scramble there must have been to come up with the substitute candidate in time for the advertised date.

However, I continued to serve as the stake Young Men president, and when the second counselor in the stake presidency moved, the stake president started to use me informally as a counselor. Then, when stake conference came, I overheard a somewhat heated discussion between the president and the visiting General Authority in which my name was mentioned. The conference came and went, and the second counselor's chair remained empty. Once again I had no trouble imagining exactly what had happened.

However, three months later the stake was divided, and I was sustained as second counselor. I was amazed and could only conclude that the Brethren had yielded to the stake president's importunity, doubtless charging him to keep a close supervisory eye on me.

A year and a half later, when the stake presidency was reorganized, I was confident that the first counselor, an excellent, well-organized man would succeed to the post. Elder Boyd K. Packer was the visiting authority, and although I had always admired him, I knew he had the reputation of being one of the more conservative of the Brethren.

I believe many were surprised when I was chosen as the stake president, but none more than I.

In order to check my perspective, I, as president, went back in the minutes of the stake presidency to see whether I had been right about what had happened. I wasn't. I had never been nominated for bishop. When I later asked the former president why not, he answered, "Why would I do that? I was grooming you to be my replacement." He also told me that the heated exchange I had assumed was over my appointment to the counselor's spot had nothing to do with me. The president had not submitted the nomination to Salt Lake City in advance, feeling that with a General Authority scheduled to attend the conference it would not be necessary. He was told that that was not the way to proceed and that he needed to send in the paper work and wait three months until the stake division for his new counselor.

The "blackball" had been a figment of my imagination. I had suffered needlessly. Yet I suppose it does not matter very much if the trial of one's faith is based on a real or only a fancied issue. There is value in the experience.

The seven years I served as president of the Cerritos California Stake were among the most satisfying of my life. I am not certain how others would characterize my presidency but my own goals were: 1) to focus the teaching and preaching and testifying in the stake on the Savior and his mission, 2) to establish scriptural scholarship at the expense of creative theology, and 3) to govern by the handbook and to do all within my power to encourage the other leaders in the stake to do likewise.

When the letter came informing me of my imminent release (it came a year sooner than I had hoped, but this time I resisted the temptation to interpret the move), I recommended myself to the Los Angeles Temple presidency as an ordinance worker and called the brother teaching the

Gospel Doctrine class in my ward to the high council. These two responsibilities, I knew, would provide the structured opportunities for spiritual feeding that I would need to deal with the withdrawal symptoms associated with no longer being the stake president.

These have been the main currents in my life as I have striven to integrate and coordinate my intellectual and my spiritual life, but of course there have been many points at which the struggle has been joined over the years. Among them are these:

THE CHURCH'S POLICY OF BLACKS NOT BEING PERMITTED TO HOLD THE PRIESTHOOD

During the years that this policy prevailed in the Church, I had many very difficult confrontations with friends and acquaintances, both black and white, who could not understand how I could support a church that promulgated such doctrine. My only answer then and now is that the priesthood belongs to God, not to me or mankind. He is not accountable to me as to how he uses it and distributes it. His ways are just, but he has never explained, so far as I know, the basis of his former policy or of its change. I am grateful, personally, to live in the time of universal access to priesthood blessings.

SUCCESSION IN THE FIRST PRESIDENCY

It has sometimes been painful for me to see the struggle that some of the General Authorities have had in performing their duties in the face of overwhelming illness, weariness, and old age. I have often wondered whether a policy that permitted members of the Twelve and the First Presidency to retire when they can no longer function would not be kinder and more effective. I confess that I am one who, at the time when President McKay was lingering beyond his ability to function, wondered aloud whether this was the Lord's means of protecting Joseph Fielding

Smith from the burdens of that onerous office, and I more recently wondered also about a similar function in President Kimball's extended illness. However, when President Smith survived to take the mantle of the prophet, I was given a surging testimony that the Lord was the architect of that transition (as did everyone who was attuned to the Spirit at that time). More recently I have had a witness that President Ezra Taft Benson was elected by the Lord, not by chance. On another occasion I remember deciding that it was not kind of the Saints to keep President Kimball alive with their prayers and decided to be courageous enough to take a more enlightened approach and pray for the Lord to take him home. I experienced such a darkness of spirit on that occasion that I will never make that mistake again.

I still do not pretend to understand why the Lord uses this system rather than others I could recommend, but I have a perfect faith that at this point it is his will that is being done.

EVOLUTION

From my youth forward, it has been clear to me that a Latter-day Saint is required to believe that Adam and Eve were real people from whom we are all descended. Beyond that I have felt that we know next to nothing about the creation of the earth or its calendar. I think it presumptuous for someone who could not repair his own TV set to think that he understands how the universe was put into operation. As I understand it, the Lord has promised to reveal more about this at some future time (see D&C 121:28–31). In the meantime I am content to have geologists and biologists put together the information available to them according to the best models they can devise. When the full truth is revealed it will encompass all that is real, not merely all that is in the understanding of a particular person or group of persons. If dinosaurs were some cruel hoax, would God have buried so many in Utah?

HOMOSEXUALITY

I think that I am as knowledgeable about the condition we call homosexuality as any heterosexual in the Church. My life has brought me into close association with many fine people whom, fortunately, I had the privilege of knowing well before I knew of their sexual orientation. My professional activities have led me to be a student of the research on this condition. As a priesthood leader and as a therapist I have worked with many people over the years as they have struggled with difficulties they face in resolving the tensions between the homosexual lifestyle and the gospel path. No one knows what determines that one individual will be drawn toward members of his own sex and another to the opposite sex. There is beginning to be some evidence that there may be a biochemical factor. Perhaps certain life experiences make the opposite sex seem more dangerous and less attractive to some than to others. Whatever the origins, I have never met a homosexual who remembered *choosing* to be so oriented. Each experiences it as an unbidden affliction.

Given that premise, it has nevertheless been my observation that those who act on those unbidden feelings lose the Spirit and before they know it are pulled step by step into a world at complete odds with the Kingdom. Those who earnestly seek to conform to the Plan are provided small miracle after small miracle until they are able to experience every blessing of the gospel. I have yet to find an exception to this rule. This puts me at odds with both those who treat men and women with homosexual feelings as though they were voluntary perverts and also with those who insist that there can be no genuine reconciliation between such persons and the highest standards of the Kingdom.

CHURCH HISTORY WITH AND WITHOUT WARTS

I am impressed with the enormous amount of scholarship that has, in recent years, provided us with a far more textured picture of our history. I am not always equally impressed with the intellectual honesty of those writing some of that history. I have always believed that whatever is true should not be flinched from. But I am often appalled at the criterion for truth that some embrace. It is fashionable these days to portray Joseph Smith as a charismatic leader who, however, did have a certain tendency for creative thinking and sexual adventurism. When I read such historical accounts I always check the footnotes. It is not too surprising to find that the evidence for these "historical" conclusions is the testimony of those who hated him and did all in their power to destroy him. It does not seem to me to be good historical practice to present such material as though it were true rather than merely alleged. Indeed, many of these allegations were made in Joseph's lifetime. Concerning those who made them, the Lord made a number of uncomplimentary and cautionary declarations (see D&C 121:11–20). Out of my own experience with the Spirit of the Lord I *know* that Joseph could not have done the salacious and self-serving things they said he did with the motivations they ascribed to him because if he had, he would have been deserted by the Spirit and replaced by one who would keep a pure heart.

In a similar vein, I find any analysis of post-Manifesto polygamy suspect, which accepts the self-serving claims of those facing Church courts at face value while placing no value at all on the testimony of the men in the First Presidency. I would not mind if they cited both and let the reader make up his own mind as to whom to believe, but I object to their taking one set as the truth and the other as the lie in their presentation.

At the beginning of this article I suggested that I have attempted to achieve my mother's faith and my stepfather's scholarship. I have been richly blessed by both pursuits, but of the two, faith is at my core, rooted in my most unchallengeable experiences. Scholarship is my most valued auxiliary. Through it my mind is enriched, my relationships enlivened, my living procured, and such worldly reputation as I have, sustained. But I never forget that when the Savior greets me at the veil, it will not be my scholarship that will be examined.

CHAPTER THREE

Midlife Report

Early in my tenure as stake president I got a call from the *Ensign* magazine asking me to do a piece aimed at middle-aged members of the Church. It seemed that President Spencer W. Kimball had noticed that most of the articles were aimed at younger families with children still at home, and though that was an important segment of Church membership, it wasn't the only group we should be trying to reach. I agreed to do it, mostly out of the long developed habit of not turning down any Church assignment. But to be perfectly honest, the topic did not move me. Every time I tried to think about it I drew a blank. What did one say to middle-aged Mormons? Finally the deadline they gave me came and went, and I sheepishly called the editor and apologized that I had let him down, but what with the demands of the stake presidency and all . . . There was a silence on the other end of the line, then, "Brother Broderick, let me put it to you this way: since he has been President of the Church, President Kimball has made only two requests of the *Ensign*. This is one of them." I said, "I'll have something in the mail for you by tomorrow." Then I had to think what it would be. Here is what I wrote.

Beginnings and endings are nearly always ceremoniously noted, but middles often pass unacknowledged. Last summer I experienced a full-fledged celebration of the middle—my twenty-fifth-year college reunion. No graduation ceremony or retirement party could have marked a life transition more convincingly.

I went, still clinging to an image of myself as an only slightly updated and improved model of the senior that I was twenty-five years before. The illusion withered before the unrelenting evidence. Everywhere I looked, the tokens of middle age assaulted my senses—receding hairlines, bulging waistlines, wrinkled brows. Even the cut of the clothing and the number of people carrying an air of confidence, of authority, witnessed that a quarter of a century had come and gone. Some wore the years more gracefully than others. Many seemed to carry their biographies boldly sketched upon their faces—the weaknesses, the strengths, the successes, and the failures.

More sobering than the faces of the living, though, were the names of the dead. As the roll of deceased classmates was read, the chapel bell tolled in cadence. Never have I felt my own mortality more starkly.

Not all of the affair was grim, of course—quite the opposite. For me the high point was the reunion with my three college roommates. As seniors, we had written out solemn predictions of what our lives would be in twenty-five years, and now we took them out and compared the prophecies against the reality.

Some things were far, far off the mark. One roommate had predicted that he would marry the girl he was then engaged to and become a corporate lawyer like his father. As it turned out, he had married a different girl and gone into the ministry. Another, having been admitted to medical school, predicted that he would become an obstetrician and operate a womens clinic in a large western city. Instead, he had become a cancer researcher in an eastern medical school and hadn't delivered a baby since his days as an intern.

I was not displeased with the match between my own foretelling and the record. My childhood sweetheart did, indeed, become my bride, and we had our predicted seven children (plus one). My career had closely followed the outline I had anticipated, and, as I had foretold, my wife and I had remained active—and busy—in the Church. As each of us read our predictions aloud and reported on our actual achievements, I had a strong feeling that this constituted, in effect, a midlife report on our personal stewardships.

As I have reflected on this in subsequent weeks, I have concluded that probably everyone needs an opportunity to evaluate his or her life in the middle. Everyone's situation is different and each person's set of stewardships may be unique, but there are five areas in which we midlifers might profitably evaluate our performance as we plan for the fiftieth reunion.

SELF

It seems to me that our first and most important stewardship is ourselves. As Latter-day Saints we have a different perspective on this than most. We are aware that our personal histories go back not to our birth into mortality but to the dawn of preearthly time. There is evidence that many, and perhaps all of us, had achieved dignity, knowledge, grace, goodness, and power long before we were ever born mortally.

Over the years I have had the privilege of giving blessings to many people as I have confirmed them, set them apart to positions, or administered to the sick, and I am often in awe of the person's spirit self, which I am permitted to glimpse through spiritual eyes.

It makes me wonder about my own spirit self. When the scales fall from my eyes and I see myself for who I was during the ages of premortal life, and compare that to who I have become, will I feel betrayed or grateful? Will I find that I have treated myself with dignity and respect and, above all, that I have come back safely to my Father?

Midlife seems like a good time to assess direction and

progress while, with a little luck, I may yet have time to improve my record.

MARRIAGE

I have also been married twenty-five years. In that I feel a triple stewardship. First, have I learned the patriarchal principle? I don't mean have I learned to dominate my wife; that is Satan's version of the principle. I mean, rather, have I learned to love her as Christ loved the Church (see Ephesians 5:25–29), preferring her above myself, exercising leadership through patience and love unfeigned, rejecting coercion, compulsion, or prideful contest as strategies of leadership (see D&C 121:41–43)?

Second, how have I guarded and nurtured our intimate relationship? When Adam and Eve became aware of their nakedness in the Garden of Eden, they fashioned aprons of leaves for themselves (see Genesis 3:7). I have often thought that those aprons symbolized our stewardship regarding our sexual nature. On the one hand they represent modesty, chastity, and fidelity. On the other hand, in their green aliveness they suggest creation and vitality. How do we fare in this double-edged stewardship? How close do we come to Paul's high standard of marital union? In our affection, have we become truly one flesh (see Ephesians 5:31)?

Third, how seriously have I taken my assignment to preside over our return to the Lord's presence? And what am I doing on a daily and weekly basis to help my wife get to know her true self? What are my immediate steps in pursuing this project in the next period of our joint stewardship?

CHILDREN

Some believe that they create their children, that they shape them out of unformed clay. Others believe that they own their children. We, however, understand how far from the truth they are on both counts. Our children are not ours. They belong to their Father in Heaven and to themselves. Our noble brothers and sisters, matured adults who agreed to become helpless babes entrusted to our care, have a right to expect us to treat them well.

By middle age we have already fulfilled most of our direct temporal responsibilities for some of our children. They have left home as independent adults, and our interaction with them may be minimal. Others of our children may be still in that not-quite-adult stage, which is often difficult for both generations.

I used to believe that if parents could just get their children on missions and into temple marriages they had demonstrated their effectiveness as stewards over their children's development. As I have seen more of life, however, I have come to realize that in many cases this is not an accurate measure of a successful stewardship. Some children turn out well despite the parenting they receive. Others go through all of the approved steps but without acquiring internal convictions or permanent profit. In still other cases the Lord has taught me that some parents are assigned difficult stewardships. Their efforts ought to be judged not by the short-term results but by the amount of love, sacrifice, and faith they have expended.

As I look at the roles my own good parents have played in my adult life, I also realize that my opportunities to nourish my children and their children are never past.

CHURCH CALLINGS

I am persuaded that one of the reasons our Church is designed differently from others, without a paid clergy, is that the Lord knows that only through service can we learn the most important virtues. No number of sermons on charity or faith can instill either, but conscientious home teaching or visiting teaching can and does. In the normal course of Church membership, most of us hold many callings. Each provides an opportunity for service and for growth, and doubtless we will have to give a stewardship report on whether we magnified or neglected each responsibility.

Church callings, however, are secondary to our primary eternal responsibilities to self, spouse, and children. That is easy to get mixed up about. I have made it a rule to address no more than one fireside outside my own stake each month. Before I made this rule, I was seldom home on Sunday evenings. One day a good sister called up from one of the neighboring stakes and asked me to address a youth devotional to be held two or three weeks hence. I politely declined, explaining that I had already filled my available slot for the month.

She was indignant: "What are you doing that evening that could be as important as being an influence for good in the lives of four hundred young people?"

"I am staying home with my own family," I replied, and wished her well in finding a speaker.

She almost made me feel guilty, but I remembered what I was told when I was set apart to my present calling: "Inevitably there will come times of crises when both your family and your calling have urgent need for your immediate attention. Someone can always fill in for you in your Church assignment; no one can replace you in your family."

CAREER

Finally, and I place it last despite its great importance, it seems very likely that we will have to account for the temporal employment we accepted—whether as homemaker or carpenter, teacher or lawyer. Are we honest? Are we dedicated to doing our best? Do we treat our fellow workers with respect and charity?

These are the stewardships I thought of. Single or divorced persons, childless or retired couples may compile a different list. In each of these areas, I feel great concern for further growth, for new goal setting. I am encouraged by the things that psychologists and sociologists have discovered about the decade of life I am entering into. Study after study shows that marriages have a tendency to improve once the children leave home and the couple have time to reinvest in each other. This is a stage when many reach the peak of their careers, while others go back to school or launch a second career with new challenges. Still others, differently disposed and situated, find it a time for easing off on their careers and turning to family and church work with new enthusiasm.

For myself, I enjoy middle age. It is good to have a track record to look back on and use as a base for making midcourse corrections. And it is good to have a few blessed years ahead to plan to make things better.

In order to make best use of the opportunity, I have decided not to wait until my fiftieth reunion for my next self-evaluation. I have sealed in an envelope my best predictions of where I will be in each area of stewardship at my thirty-fifth reunion. Life takes peculiar twists and turns, and I have far less confidence in my foretelling now than I did as a brash college senior. But the exercise is still valuable. It forces self-assessment; it helps to focus priorities and goals; it reminds me of how much I have to be grateful for and that when much is given, much is expected. And it gives me practice in making stewardship reports on my life, which I suppose will one day come in handy.

CHAPTER FOUR

Summing It Up
(Or, Why Let Somebody Else
Write Your Obituary?)

It is a bit presumptuous and some would say morbid to write one's own obituary. On the other hand, I have reached the age where I am attending many more funerals than weddings, and it seems natural to me to start thinking about one's mortality and to do a sort of life review at this point. Although Kathleen and I are looking forward to our retirement from the University in a couple of years and going on the mission we missed in our youth, at the moment that I wrote this I was in the midst of a health crisis that cast some shadow on whether or not we would be permitted to fulfill that plan. Happily, the crisis passed, but the opportunity it provoked for a serious life review was valuable.

Lives have themes, and in retrospect, I could say that the most meaningful themes of my life have been these: From the beginning I was a performer and an educator; as I matured, I became a healer and a patriarch.

Performer: I think I came by this genetically. I never knew my paternal relatives (and barely remember my father, since my mother divorced him when I was only one and a half years old and he dropped out of my life altogether a very few years after that). So I have no idea of their contribution to my genetic propensities, but my mother and her father were natural performers. By the time I was six, I was already volunteering to be the "minuteman" to fill in for the children who had forgotten their assigned 2-1/2 minute talks for Sunday School opening exercises. I remember on one occasion having to be manhandled from the podium because I was telling the story of Joseph who was sold into Egypt, and I was already running ten minutes over with no end in sight. I never had the voice for serious solo work, but I was in a choir every year of my life from fifth grade through about age forty (when I got too busy with other things), and I never shrank from a solo or duet if it was musical comedy rather than inspirational music that was needed. I was in a quartet in high school—The Flapjack Four—and we did the Kiwanian circuit. But my biggest thrills were found in stage shows: *The Mikado*, in high school (I played Pooh Bah), and in later years in State College, Pennsylvania, where I played the father in the Amish musical *Plain and Fancy* and the lawyer in *Mame*. In still later years, in Cerritos, California, I was in almost every stake road show, some years as the music director, every year as a performer. In the '70s I was on the *Tonight Show* with Jonny Carson ten times, masquerading as an expert on marriage and sex, but always going for a better audience response than the host.

Educator: As a kid I thought I knew everything, and I was nothing loath to share my knowledge. Two incidents come to mind. When I was ten I was sent home from Sunday School because I had explained to the class what "Thou shalt not commit adultery" meant. (It was clear to me from her explanation that the teacher didn't have a clue.) That same year, at YMCA summer camp, I got into a scripturally documented hour-long discussion on religion with another boy, which earned me the nickname "Moses." In high school, Kathleen's affectionate nickname for me was "Professor," and at church they had me teaching the seventeen-year-olds in Sunday School while I was still that age myself. Over the years I have learned (sometimes painfully) the limits of my erudition, but I have never given up teaching or, as some would say, teaching-performing. That has been my secular profession, and whatever my Church calling, I always found some way of turning it into a teaching situation. For example, only a year or two after I became a temple worker, I was called to be a trainer, and I think most who worked closely with me while I served as stake president would agree that that was the aspect of the job that I most enjoyed (I did my best to delegate most of the rest to my counselors).

Healer: One who knew my family might argue that I came by this talent as naturally as I inherited my penchant for performing. My maternal grandmother was a nurse, and my mother was a world-class natural healer of the unlovables of this world. But, although I suppose I was generally a cheerful and prosocial person all my life, as a young person I had no particular sensitivity to others' pain nor insight into their circumstances. Whatever healing arts I ultimately may have acquired came to me through professional and Church service opportunities during my adult years. I shall be eternally grateful for the opportunities that I have been provided to assist in the healing process in the lives of a number of remarkable persons. In many cases it has been a very personal encounter. In others, it has been over the podium or through books or articles. My patriarchal blessing promised me that I would write literature that would bless, and many individuals over the years have been kind enough to let me know that in their case, that was fulfilled. Few things could be more satisfying.

Patriarch: I don't remember when it became clear to me, some time in my late thirties or early forties, that my greatest contribution on this earth would be as a father to remarkable children (within the extraordinary partnership of my quite incomparable marriage). It was never Kathleen's or my challenge to wrestle with rebellious spirits. Ours intuitively loved what was good and true and righteous from the beginning. All they required was teaching. They were eager, even demanding learners. They will be eager and demanding teachers of their own children. In proud moments, I think of Kathleen and me as founders of a dynasty of committed parents and spiritual leaders. To have been called to the office of patriarch in the Church in my mature years is the cherry on the (chocolate) patriarchal sundae.

My children know that I know and love the Lord and am committed to serve him to the end. They know that I am a witness of the restoration of the gospel of Jesus Christ through the instrumentality of Joseph Smith, that I love the scriptures, modern and ancient, and support the Brethren with a full heart. They know that second only to this knowledge, my greatest gift to them is their incomparable mother and the seamless love we have for each other and for them.

PART II

Some Incidental Observations on Mormon Marriages

CHAPTER FIVE

But What if Your Husband Is a Jerk!?

The editor of the *Ensign* called to ask me if I could do a piece responding to a letter they had received from a sister who, in effect, asked for guidance on when and whether a good LDS wife was justified in setting some limits on her husband's behavior (rather than being charitable and long-suffering). He and his staff felt that the topic was an important one and that I was just the person to address it. I was enthusiastic about the assignment because the issue comes up regularly in therapy, and there was really nothing written on it from an LDS perspective. The substance of this good sister's letter is included in the opening paragraphs of the article. I loved her closing line, "But what if your husband is a jerk!?" and used it as the title of the article. In this case, I'm sure I beat the deadline by several weeks.

The editor phoned me to indicate that they had received the piece and that it was exactly what they had asked me to do . . . [I could hear the "but" coming], *but* some of the staff felt it wasn't quite in keeping with the spirit of the *Ensign*. I said I'd be willing to change the title. They'd get back to me, he said. Weeks and months passed. I'd already circulated a preprint copy among some LDS colleagues and clients with enthusiastic response, so I was anxious to get the piece into circulation. I called the magazine and learned that they were still hopeful that they could use a couple of key paragraphs from it. So I asked for it back and sent it to *This People* magazine where it was ultimately published.

The sister who gave the lesson somehow managed to communicate the fact, without saying so, that she had lived the principle she taught. Her subject had been the responsibility of wives to be patient with their husbands' imperfections. Men, she acknowledged, often had the tendency to be too much influenced by the World and too little by the Spirit. Often they were insensitive and unappreciative. The remedy was neither to give up on them nor to try to make them over into something finer. Rather, the spiritually underdeveloped spouse ought to be led by unconditional love and a good example to see the better path.

Various sisters responded differently to the message. Certain ones nodded wisely, serene in the confirmation of their own conviction. Others sighed and added the burden of repentance in this thing to their already full measure of challenges. But one outspoken young woman came up afterward to express a view shared by some others who lacked the courage to voice it. "Patience and forgiveness are okay to a point," she said, "but what if your husband is a jerk!?"

The question, though inelegantly phrased, is a profoundly important one. What if your husband really *is* a jerk? What if living with him is spiritually toxic and demeaning? Is it righteous counsel to advise wives (or husbands, for that matter) to set no limits on a spouse's bad behavior? Isn't there in fact some point beyond which one passes from being a patient wife to being a consenting victim of physical and emotional abuse; from being a loyal and nonjudgmental mate to being an accessory to dishonest business dealings, sexual immorality, or child abuse?

The trick, of course, is not in agreeing that there must be such a point, but to identify it clearly in one's own situation. Are there righteous principles that can guide one in the decision that this far is too far?

Perhaps a few examples may serve to raise some of these issues.

Carol was a widow with a fifteen-year-old daughter. Carol decided to marry a charming, faithful member of the Church whom she had met some months earlier at a singles function. Jack had three teenage boys, one preparing for his mission. Given their age and sex, the boys seemed reasonably well-behaved and personable. It was decided that they would sell Jack's house and move into Carol's because it was bigger and in a better neighborhood. After the marriage, there were the usual, to-be-expected hassles with getting the boys to respect her furniture, to do their fair share of the chores, and so on. It bothered her that Jack always sided with his sons rather than working with her to find solutions, but she accepted all of this with as much grace as she could, understanding that such issues are not too unusual in blended families. But certain other issues raised the question of limits with her. First, she found that the decor in the master bedroom reminded her uncomfortably of her first marriage, and as a gift to her present marriage, she determined to redecorate it, using her own money to do so. She informed Jack of her plan, expecting him to be pleased about it, and was shocked when he not only declared the idea stupid and neurotic but *forbad* her doing it. She was not accustomed to being forbidden to decorate her own home.

About the same time, her young daughter asked for a lock to be installed on her bedroom door. No one had actually disturbed her privacy, but she felt exposed and insecure with all of the new male presences in the house. She thought a lock would help her feel more secure. This seemed a reasonable request to her mother, but her stepfather was mortally offended at the implication that she was less safe with him and his sons than she was before. Again, he forbad his wife to install any such affront to his family's morals. In this case, she felt that her daughter's comfort should prevail, and Carol installed the lock herself one day while Jack was at work. When he discovered it, he ripped it out of the door, cursing her and her daughter, whom he characterized as paranoid and neurotic, in front of the assembled family.

There were other, similar incidents that had the cumulative effect of making this woman feel that somehow, by her marrying, she and her daughter had become an oppressed minority in their own home. Most would agree, her husband was being "a real jerk." Question: Would she be justified in doing something about it, and if so, what?

Let us look at a second real-life case. Anna had a temple marriage, but despite this, discovered that her husband was addicted to pornography. Soon after their honeymoon he began bringing home sexually explicit videos, pressuring her to join him in watching them. He also thought that a little wine would loosen up her inhibitions and that the combination would add immeasurably to their sex life. Sometimes he hinted that if she altogether refused him in this he would be driven to meet his needs elsewhere. (Of course, this would be her fault, if it happened, since it didn't need to be that way if she would only loosen up and *try* it his way.) Anna mentioned her dilemma to a girlfriend at work who assured her that men were just like that and that if you could learn to please them in bed it made everything else go a lot better. "Hey," she said, "you might even get to like it."

Latter-day Saints, at least, would agree that her husband was being "a real jerk." Question: What should she do?

There is an enormous variety of ways to be offensive in marriage, but we will consider one final example. Cindy admitted that she was stubborn and had a temper. The trouble was that so did her husband, Phil. She had grown up in a family that argued and then made up afterward, and that pattern seemed pretty normal to her. But her father had never, in all those years of arguments, ever physically attacked her mother, so Cindy was totally unprepared when, in the midst of a fierce debate, Phil told her to just shut up and when she didn't, he hit her hard enough to knock her across the room. Then he stomped out of the house and drove around until he had calmed down. Later, he said he was really sorry, but that she drove him to it, and besides, he had really only shoved her, not actually hit her with his fist. Afterward he said he really loved her and promised he'd never do it again, and they made up—just like her folks always did after a quarrel.

But it did happen again. In fact, it became a regular cycle. They would quarrel, he would hit her, and then he'd leave till he calmed down. He would come home and beg her forgiveness, promise not to do it again, and they would make up. A few times he really hurt her, and she had to have stitches taken. But mostly, he just humiliated and frightened her. Sometimes she thought that if it were only the two of them, she could handle it, but as the children got older, they would be awakened by the racket, and she hated them being exposed to this kind of violence. Thinking how it might affect the children, that was the worst of it for her. She considered going to the bishop about it and almost mentioned it in a temple recommend interview, but her husband and the bishop were good friends and hunting buddies, and she just couldn't bring herself to do it. A few times Cindy thought of leaving Phil, but she had three little children and nowhere to go—and besides, at heart she knew she really loved this jerk she was married to. Question: What should she do? What *could* she do?

Considering these women's dilemmas (and all of the similar ones we haven't the space to illustrate), several things seem clear. *First,* these women have legitimate complaints. None of them are perfect wives, and it is probable that each contributed to the problem she faced, but none deserved the response she got. Each of these husbands crossed the line from acceptable to unacceptable behavior. *Second,* none of these men showed any inclination to change their behavior. In fact, each basically blamed his wife for his actions, taking no responsibility for them himself, never coming close to honestly repenting. *Third,* it appears that if she does nothing to change the pattern, it will continue, and she will become, through her inaction, an accomplice to it. *Fourth,* marriage vows are among the most sacred a man or woman can make, but one is *not* required to participate in humiliating subjugation, sin, or abuse to honor them. In fact, by perpetuating such behavior or submitting to it, the parties dishonor both their vows and the God before whom they were taken.

Several gospel principles seem to apply. These occur to me. You may think of others.

1) The Lord cares about the plight of women and children who are abused physically or spiritually by their husbands and fathers. The Book of Mormon prophet Jacob was addressing families whose fathers had committed the particular sin of adultery, but the principle applies to any serious offense:

> For behold, I, the Lord, have seen the sorrow, and heard the mourning of the daughters of my people . . . because of the wickedness and abominations of their husbands. And I will not suffer, saith the Lord of Hosts, that the cries of the fair daughters of this people . . . shall come up unto me against the men of my people, saith the Lord of Hosts. . . . Behold, ye have done greater iniquities than the Lamanites, our brethren. Ye have broken the hearts of your tender wives, and lost the confidence of your children, because of your bad examples before them. (Jacob 2:31–32, 35)

2) Although the Lord counsels patience and long-suffering in the face of persecution, in the particular case when the welfare of our homes and children is at stake, he counsels us that a protective obligation sets limits on the application of that more general principle. I do not believe it stretches the parallels unduly to apply the advice he gave the

Nephites when they were struggling to protect their families and their right to worship and obey the God of their fathers:

> *They were not fighting for monarchy nor power but they were fighting for their homes and their liberties, their wives and their children, and their all, yea, for their rites of worship and their church. And they were doing that which they felt was the duty which they owed to their God; for the Lord had said unto them . . . that: Inasmuch as ye are not guilty of the first offense, neither the second, ye shall not suffer yourselves to be slain by the hands of your enemies [but] . . . ye shall defend your families.* (Alma 43:45–47)

3) Clearly, there is an obligation to make every effort to resolve the problem within the marriage. Counsel from priesthood leaders should be sought, and, if it seems appropriate, professional counseling from a competent therapist who shares your values might be helpful. Often these interventions may lead your husband to reconsider his ways. It is an unhappy truth that sometimes nothing seems to help, and he may persist in his offensive behavior. The Savior counseled the Church on what its course of action ought to be toward those whose offensive behavior threatens the integrity of the Church. Again, it does not seem to me to be stretching the parallel to apply this guideline to the family:

> *Ye shall not [initially] cast him out from among you, but ye shall minister unto him and shall pray for him unto the Father, in my name; and if it so be that he repenteth . . . then shall ye receive him, . . . But if he repent not he shall not be numbered among my people, that he may not destroy my people.* (3 Nephi 18:30–31)

Paul elaborates on the conditions that justify breaking up a marriage faithfully entered into:

> *Be ye not unequally yoked together with unbelievers: for what fellowship hath righteousness with unrighteousness? and what communion hath light with darkness? And what concord hath Christ with Belial? or what part hath he that*

*believeth with an infidel? And what agreement hath the
temple of God with idols? for ye are the temple of the living
God; as God hath said, I will dwell in them, and walk in
them; and I will be their God, and they shall be my people.
Wherefore come out from among them, and be ye separate,
saith the Lord, and touch not the unclean thing; and I will
receive you. And will be a Father unto you, and ye shall
be my sons and daughters, saith the Lord Almighty.*
(2 Corinthians 6:14–18)

All of us find things in our spouses that we do not appreciate and that we wish were different. Perhaps most of us
could find areas where genuine spousal repentance would
be in order (leaving aside for the moment our own failings).
Most of us understand that marriage is a matter of give and
take, of forbearance and forgiveness. But there are limits. *But
there are limits.* Without limits there is no human dignity, no
protection against the influence of the adversary in our
homes. With the help of the Spirit and inspired counsel, we
can determine what those limits need to be in our own
situation—and what to do if those limits are exceeded.

CHAPTER SIX

Marital Danger Zones

Since dealing with marital problems is what I do for a living, you probably would think that an invitation from *This People* magazine to "do a piece for us on avoiding marriage problems" wouldn't be much of a challenge. On the other hand, remember that I have already written a college text, *Marriage and the Family,* a secular trade book, *Couples,* and a book for Church members, *One Flesh, One Heart,* plus any number of articles on the subject for various magazines and books. It is not that easy to come up with a piece that says something worth reading that you haven't already addressed in one of the above. Then if you think about all of the other people in the field and the hundreds of books and thousands of articles they have written, well, fresh material isn't that easy to come by. And even if you can think of a worthwhile idea that hasn't been gone over a hundred times, try coming up with a title that is engaging and descriptive and not yet thread-bare from overuse.

Happily, in this case, when the invitation from *This People* arrived in the mail, I had just come back from the annual meetings of the American Association for Marriage and Family Therapy where I had heard John Gottman report on his wonderfully informative longitudinal study of what makes marriages tick (or quit ticking) (John M. Gottman, *What Predicts Divorce? The Relationship between Marital Processes and Marital Outcomes* [Minneapolis: National Council on Family Relations], 1995). The Gottman report had stimulated my thinking about an idea that I had often found useful in counseling married couples but had never gotten around to writing up. So I had the content; but what about a title? We (the editors and I) eventually settled on "Marital Danger Zones," mainly because it was an eye-catcher and because I couldn't think of an equally good title that conveyed the idea of shifting marital gears. In any case, here it is.

The sensor taped to his palm showed that his hands were starting to sweat, his blood pressure was creeping up, and his heartbeat was beginning to reflect his rising level of stress. On the video monitor the experimenters could see that he was growing red in the face as his wife persisted:

Michael, listen to what I'm saying; this is important! The romance has gone from our marriage . . . gone . . . I don't know where, but it's going, going, gone! We never talk to each other about our feelings anymore, we never . . . Michael, are you listening to me?

According to the stress indicators, his level of discomfort is easing off a little. The observers note that his eyes have glazed over, and he appears to be focused on some fixed point just over his wife's left shoulder. The female observer turns to her male colleague and remarks, "Oh-oh! She's taken out after him, and he's retreated into never-never land."

They recognize the signs. This couple has just passed into the "Marital Danger Zone."

Five years of longitudinal research has shown that if this pattern becomes established as a regular feature of their "intimate discussions," they will find themselves in the highest-risk category for marital breakup. It is hard to say whether it is the husband's entrenched avoidance or the wife's dogged pursuit that starts the cycle. It is clear, however, that it takes both to keep it going to its final, maritally fatal end. The more he avoids engaging with her in "meaningful discussions," the more she provokes such an engagement. I have known at least one man to lock himself in the bathroom to escape, only to have his wife take the hinges off the door to get at him.

Eventually, of course, she gets disgusted with his refusing to involve himself in serious communication with her. At this point, *she* withdraws, "having done everything it was possible to do to make this marriage work." In this kind of deteriorating relationship, it is most often she who initiates the separation and eventual divorce.

There may actually be a biological basis for this pattern. Just as men, on the average, are bigger and stronger than their wives and will usually end up inflicting the most damage in a violent brawl, so women are advantaged in verbal-emotional exchanges and can usually get the best of their male partner in contests of this type. Some years ago, it was discovered that women, on the average, have 25 to 50 percent more neural connectors between the feeling centers of the right brain and the verbal centers of the left brain than do men. So, when a woman wants to have a deep discussion with her husband on matters of vital importance to their marriage, and, for starters, she asks him to tell her exactly how he feels about their relationship, and he says, "I feel fine about it," and she says, "No, I want you to open up and share your deepest feelings with me, your fears, your disappointments, your hopes, your dreams," and he says, "Well, it would be nice to have sex a little more often," and that's all she can get out of him, it may be more than selfish, hormonally driven, stubborn noncooperation on his part. We may be dealing here, literally, with a deficit in his hard-wiring.

There is, of course, a certain inequity in this arrangement. In our culture, women daily use their biological advantage with society's full approval, while men who use their advantage go to jail, or at least end up in a meaningful interview with the bishop. But that's beyond the scope of this discussion.

The key, however, lies not in the biological inequality.

Men can (and most men do) live together peacefully with physically smaller and weaker mates, never allowing their differences of opinion to escalate into a violent free-for-all. Women can (and most women do) live together with emotionally inarticulate mates without resorting to the kind of relentless attack to which Michael was subjected in the earlier paragraph. The key lies in an attitude, not in a difference. Every couple has differences in strengths of every kind. Every couple has differences of opinion as to how the relationship might be improved. Yet, most couples (well, about half, anyway) manage to deal with these differences in ways that do not destroy the relationship. What kills marriages is *competitive contests of will.* Contests where, if he wins, she loses or where she can only triumph at his expense.

In this type of marriage there is never a shared victory. And couples *need* shared victories. The competition needs to be between the couple and the outside world, not between team members.

Latter-day Saints with temple marriages are not immune to falling into the toxic trap of competition. In fact, it seems to me that they are particularly vulnerable to it. Both men and women in the Church are rewarded for being good competitors. Whether in volleyball or scripture chase or in the race to be touted in the mission newsletter as the "Top Baptizers of the Month," we are encouraged to put our all into beating the other guys. The Good Sportsmanship Trophy is not much coveted.

I am not suggesting that the Church abandon its systematic training of fierce competitors. Occasionally we are reminded by Church leaders that there might be better motivation for improved home teaching or temple attendance than a free steak dinner for the winning quorum and beans for the losers, or to show the First Ward that we can beat them in virtue just like we beat them in basketball. Initially, I am always encouraged by this renewed evidence of the Brethren's faith in the transtelestial quality of members' motivation to do good. But it never seems to work. At least in my observation, no sooner are the quotas and competitions banned than we see home teaching sag, temple attendance drop off, and district baptism rates hit new lows. In our culture, it may be that, telestial or not, the competitive value is too deeply embedded to be easily replaced by a finer, more celestial (or at least terrestrial) motivation.

Having admitted that, it remains true that between husband and wife, competition does *not* result in improved performance. All too often, it just fast-forwards the marital drama to the closing credits.

The same researchers who identified the toxic pattern of competition found that the best single-item predictor of long-term marital success among the couples they studied was "Husband voluntarily and cheerfully participates in the housework." There may be a number of reasons why this item turned out to be such a powerful predictor, but my guess is that it has to do with attitudes. The husband who pitches in to do his share without having to be cajoled is clearly a team player. His enemy is not his wife; she is his invaluable ally in the unceasing battle against the common enemy—those famous and all-too-familiar "slings and arrows of outrageous fortune."

On the surface, the dilemmas of biological inequality and misplaced competition appear to be unresolvable. Fortunately, there is a very practical solution to these and other sources of tension in marriage. This unheralded technique and its amazing effectiveness, successfully employed by countless couples who don't even know they are using it, first came to my attention in the midst of some research on a very different type of marital challenge.

Many Navy wives are faced with the necessity of adapting to the stressful duty-rotation that separates them from their husbands for six months of every year. As any single mother knows, trying to run a household without a partner can be tough. Actually, the research team was impressed with how well these temporarily single women handled the challenge. With a minimum of flailing about, virtually all of them found the means to handle the tasks that their husbands took care of when they were home. Some took over the jobs themselves; some pressed older children into service; some accepted generous offers of assistance from neighbors' husbands who were assigned to shore duty for those six months; all found a way to manage.

The far more difficult task was to move aside to make room for the husband when he came home. Suddenly, this independent woman found herself accountable to her returning warrior for how she spent her time, how she managed the family resources, whom she talked to on the phone, and how she disciplined the kids. The children found they had to deal with different (and almost always more restrictive) rules. Suddenly, they couldn't stay up as late, or stay over at their friend's place, or wear makeup. In most homes, the husband's return was anticipated with ambivalence and experienced as a period of tension and conflict.

But not in all. In a certain subset of homes, the transition was accomplished smoothly. It wasn't that the family rules didn't have to change as the husband/father reentered the family. They did. But it all happened with a minimum of resentment and contention. What was the mechanism that made it work?

One of the wives in the smooth-transition families explained it to us. "I know just what you are talking about," she said, "and it's really very simple. We have a gear shift."

"A gear shift?"

"Yes. When Daddy's away, we all operate in Sea Duty Gear, and when he's home, we all shift to Shore Duty Gear."

We checked the concept out with other members from smooth-transition families, and they agreed that was a good description of how it worked for them. Everybody recognized that there were different house rules when Dad was home. It was part of the package. As one put it, "It's like the change of seasons where I grew up. No sense in fighting it. Just put on your overcoat and boots and enjoy the good parts."

Daddy's home. *Shift.* Daddy's gone. *Shift.* Daddy's home again. *Shift again.* Everybody knows the rules. Everybody understands the need. Everybody shifts without even thinking much about it when the time comes.

That is a tremendously important idea. Once it is understood, one can see many applications in family living. At home you can get away with tearing around the house and pounding on the piano, but at Grandma's, *Shift.* New rules, and everybody knows what they are. Study after study has found that it is the flexible families, the adjustable families, the families with a built-in shift mechanism that thrive in this checkered world.

Which brings us back to how a couple can strive successfully in a competitive environment all day and leave that style behind as they approach the driveway of their own home. How can they survive among the predators in the world, living by the telestial, dog-eat-dog laws of the secular jungle, and still live in a loving, mutually supportive marriage? The answer is, learn to *shift!* If you don't, you will have no protection from the dread effects of *spillover*, which is the sociological term for bringing the world home with you.

Thoroughgoing competitors will find this difficult at first. Perhaps it has never occurred to them that there ought to be a major sphere of life where the rules of competition are set aside and the rules of cooperation apply. On the other hand, each and every one of them will have accumulated a large body of personal experience attesting to the fact that competition really doesn't work very well between marital partners.

After considering the matter soberly, many will conclude

that it is in their own best interest, and entirely within their own power, to try it the other way. For the experiment to succeed, it is a great advantage if one has had some previous experience with playing by terrestrial rules, that is, practice in being honorable, honest, kind, and considerate in an ongoing relationship. Many may never have experienced these rules in operation in the homes where they grew up, but most will have encountered them somewhere. (Notice, I say nothing of *celestial* rules. In my experience, they are not much applied anywhere in this life, except in sermons.)

Some, on reading this, will observe that they have always understood this principle, and may with justifiable pride and gratitude, mentally pat their own well-lubricated transmission box. Others (mainly women) will be very excited about sharing this article with their husbands, even if they have to take the hinges off the bathroom door to get them to read it. Still others (mostly men) will find their palms sweating and their blood pressure rising at the very broaching of the subject. I wish each and every one the lawful consequences of their own choices in the matter.

CHAPTER SEVEN

How Come Good People Can Have Bad Marriages?

When asked how he governed his people, Joseph Smith replied, "I do not govern them; I teach them true principles and they govern themselves."

Ah, were it as easy as that, folks like me would have to do honest work for a living. The reality is that virtually all of us know the correct principles; it is just that we are too blind to see their application to our own situation or too stubborn to give up our habitual unprincipled ways of doing business.

That is why the books and articles on how to make money, raise children, and do marriage keep coming out and keep finding a market. Most often, the writer's challenge is not to find some new angle, but to repackage the basic principles that have existed from before the foundation of the world.

This chapter and chapter eight are examples of that genre. Both deal with core principles that have been taught by every prophet since Adam and in every "how-to" book and article since Gutenberg invented the printing press. One I wrote in 1983, in response to a question sent by a reader to the *Ensign*. The other was written twelve years later and constituted my contribution to a book on improving marriage that included articles from a number of LDS therapists. On the face of it, the pieces are very different. At their core they are two versions of that same old refrain.

Q: *After seeing the marriage of my parents (both good, decent people) fail, I find myself questioning my attitudes toward marriage. How can I keep faith in this most important principle?*

A: Many people become disillusioned and upset when they see couples they have trusted and admired get divorced. They say to themselves, "If these couples couldn't make it, what chance do ordinary people like us have?" Often the divorcing husband and wife are just as disillusioned.

Several years ago a husband and wife, both active members of the Church, came to me professionally with very serious marital problems. Both said, "How could this be happening to us? We have a temple marriage. We have kept the commandments. We pay our tithing, keep the Word of Wisdom, attend the temple regularly, and serve the Lord faithfully in our Church callings. It just isn't fair! Why aren't we blessed with a happy marriage?"

I opened the Doctrine and Covenants and had them read verses twenty and twenty-one of Section 130:

> There is a law, irrevocably decreed in heaven before the foundations of this world, upon which all blessings are predicated—And when we obtain any blessing from God, it is by obedience to that law upon which it is predicated.

I told them that they had been blessed for keeping the laws they had obeyed but that the Lord could not bless them with a happy marriage unless they kept the laws that apply to happy marriages. "For example," I said, "you say you keep the law of tithing?"

"Actually," the husband replied, "we probably pay a little extra."

"Good. And do you receive the blessings associated with that law?"

They looked at each other. "Yes, we have been richly blessed concerning that law."

"You say you keep the Word of Wisdom?"

"Scrupulously."

"And do you receive the blessings promised to those who are obedient to that law?"

"Yes. The Lord has blessed us each with health and enough energy to do the many things we have to do."

"In exactly the same way, the Lord will bless you with a happy marriage if you keep the laws that govern happiness in marriage," I told them.

They inquired what those might be, and I referred them to Doctrine and Covenants 121:34–46 (where the Lord provides instruction in the exercise of righteous leadership) and to chapter twelve of Romans (where Paul outlines the laws governing unity in any unit of the Church).

They candidly acknowledged that despite the guidance offered in Doctrine and Covenants 121, they did not in fact exercise their joint leadership responsibilities "only by persuasion, by long-suffering, by gentleness and meekness, and by love unfeigned; By kindness, and pure knowledge . . . without hypocrisy, and without guile" (v. 42). Rather, they engaged in constant power struggles over who was right and who was wrong and used all kinds of strategies to "win" in the family arena.

They admitted also that contrary to Paul's counsel in Romans 12 their expectations of each other were all too "conformed to this world" (v. 2); that both were given to thinking of their own opinions "more highly than he ought to think" (v. 3); that there was insufficient positive appreciation for the ways they were different (see vv. 4–6); that there was a shortage in their home of mercy, cheerfulness, love, and kindly affection, "preferring one another" (vv. 8–10). They acknowledged that they had not always rejoiced when their partner rejoiced or wept when he or she wept (see v. 15); that they were often not "of the same mind one toward another" (v. 16); and that they did not strive as much as they possibly could to "live peaceably" with each other (v. 18). Finally, they confessed that they had never mastered the rule to "avenge not yourselves" instead of giving "place unto wrath" (v. 19), or to "be not overcome of evil, but overcome evil with good" (v. 21).

In short, I told them, they were in some ways in the situation of those who "pay tithe of mint and anise and cummin, and have omitted the weightier matters of the law, judgment, mercy, and faith: these ought [they] to have done, and not [left] the other undone" (Matthew 23:23).

To answer your questions directly, then, you need to know that you can be assured of a rewarding, enduring, heaven-bound marriage if you obey the laws that govern this part of life. They are among the highest and most challenging laws in all of the gospel; no other reward is so great as that promised by the Lord to those who keep them.

"For strait is the gate, and narrow the way that leadeth unto the exaltation and continuation of the lives, and few there be that find it, . . . But if ye receive me in the world, then shall ye know me, and shall receive your exaltation; that where I am ye shall be also" (D&C 132:22–23).

CHAPTER EIGHT

Eternal
Surviving ^ Marriage

I had lunch once with two old friends: one a Protestant minister, who ran one of the campus religious centers, and the other a member of the faculty of the law school. The conversation drifted to the topic of of lawyer-bashing jokes. Among the more elaborate examples offered (by the minister, in this case) was the following:

> A very much in love young couple were on their way to the wedding chapel to be united in holy matrimony, and only a few dozen yards from their destination, they were hit by a truck and were killed. At the Pearly Gates, St. Peter offered to grant them the standard righteous-desire-of-their-hearts. He was taken aback, however, when they insisted in a single voice that they had only one desire and that was to complete the wedding ceremony that they had been so rudely and unjustly cheated out of. St. Peter tried to explain that they were making a highly irregular—even improper—request. There was no marrying or giving in marriage in heaven . . . it just wasn't done. But they were adamant. Heaven wouldn't be heaven unless they could be together, et cetera, et cetera. Finally, St. Peter said, "Okay, okay, I'll check into it, but this may take some doing, so be patient." But they were not patient. Every day they checked two or three

times to see if any progress had been made toward granting their desire. Each time, Peter said, "I'm working on it, I'm working on it." Finally, after three seemingly endless weeks of intense longing, the good news came. It had been arranged.

The ceremony was lovely, but simple—just the minister, the two of them, and St. Peter and one other angel, who served as witnesses. Afterwards they set up housekeeping in their own heavenly love nest. But things did not go well. Small disappointments and disagreements escalated into major quarrels. Major quarrels escalated into knock-down, drag-out fights. After only a few weeks they returned to St. Peter demanding a divorce. "A divorce!" he said. "After all the trouble I had to get you married!"

"Believe me," said the man, "it wouldn't be heaven if I had to live with this shrew for eternity!" "I demand my rights to personal privacy and peace," said the woman, "and I don't get a moment of either with this monster. I demand a divorce!"

St. Peter looked at them for a long moment. "You really don't know what you're asking," he said, shaking his head wearily. "It took me three weeks to find a minister up here. Do you have any idea how long it will take me to find a lawyer?"

It was a clever joke on three counts: It zinged the minister who told it; it double-zinged the lawyer; and even more slyly, it triple-zinged the third member of the group, who was known to be a Mormon and an advocate of the doctrine of eternal marriage. The point scored all too painfully. How often have I heard those very words from couples sealed for time and all eternity in the temples of our God (closer to the "Pearly Gates" than the storyteller could imagine). "It just wouldn't be the celestial kingdom if I had to be tied to this miserable person for all eternity." Secular divorce rates stabilized at an all-time high in about 1979. Divorce rates for temple marriages, historically several times lower than secular rates, have continued to climb, gradually narrowing the gap that separates the two. The current survival rate for temple marriages is not overly impressive.

Often I have asked myself why this is so. Latter-day Saints know the principles of eternal unity. I am persuaded that there is no principle of successful marital life that I could share with good LDS couples that would be new to them. In fact, any principle that purported to be true and crucial to successful living that was new to them should be immediately suspect. The laws governing marital satisfaction are but special applications of the laws of the gospel, and every good Latter-day Saint learned them in Primary (or, in the case of converts, in the six missionary discussions and the twelve Gospel Essentials classes). The problem seems to come in making the special applications from general gospel principles to the specific marital situation.

The point was vividly illustrated in a recent experience I had with a colleague. He is Jewish and one of the finest family therapists I know. I have referred close friends and relatives to him with good results. One day a woman called me to see if she could make an appointment to bring in her family for some counseling. Their problem was a rebellious teenager and an escalating power struggle between her and her parents that was getting out of hand.

Without minimizing the seriousness of this type of problem, it must be acknowledged that it is a common bread-and-butter sort of issue for family therapists. They deal with various versions of it every week. Both research and common observation have shown that when kids get into trouble, it is generally a case of too little supervision and too few consequences for breaking family rules, or, equally often, a case of too many rigid rules and overly strict and intrusive enforcement leading to rebellion. In the first case the therapist works with the family to set up a more structured home environment. In the second case the therapist works with the family to unwind the system a little.

This family who called appeared to be of the second type. As it happened, they lived on the opposite side of Los Angeles from me and quite near my good Jewish colleague. I suggested that they might wish to save themselves the long drive and trust their problem to this excellent clinician. They agreed that this was a sensible suggestion and started to work with him.

After only a couple of weeks, I got a call from my friend. "Carl, I need some help with this couple you referred to me."

"What's the problem? They probably just need to loosen up the parental iron fist a little."

"That's right. If they don't, this kid is about to run away from home or attempt suicide or do something else drastic. But, Carl, every time I suggest any movement in the direction of loosening up, they patiently explain to me that I just don't understand their religious obligation, as Mormon parents, to keep this kid in line. Frankly, I don't know how to deal with this. I don't want to attack their religious beliefs, but the situation is explosive."

I thought a moment and then said, "Here's what you do. First, tell them that during the time you have been working with them, you have developed a real curiosity about the Mormon religion. This will serve to get their attention. Then say that there is one issue that keeps coming up when you ask about it that has you mystified. You keep hearing about some 'war in heaven,' but you can never quite figure out what it is about."

"That's it? I just ask them to explain the 'war in heaven'?"

"That's it."

"Carl, what's the war in heaven?"

"It doesn't matter; just do what I said and let me know how it goes."

A few days later he called. "Carl, I can't believe it. I did what you said, and it was like magic."

"So tell me about the session."

"Well, as you suggested, I told them that since I started working with them I had gotten sort of interested in the Mormon religion. You wouldn't believe the response. Even the rebellious teenage kid promised to give me a copy of some book on the Church with the family picture in the front. Then I said there was just one thing that kind of confused me about their beliefs. I kept hearing about a war in heaven. What was this war in heaven? Well, the mom didn't as much as take a minute to collect her thoughts. In seconds she had launched into some story about a council in heaven and two plans and she gets about three minutes into it and she stops cold in her tracks and gives me a funny look and says, 'All right, Doctor, you've made your point.' From that moment on they were like putty in my hands. It was like magic. Carl, what is this war in heaven?"

Of course, there was no magic. This good LDS woman simply had the unnerving experience of explaining Satan's plan to an "investigator" and, in the midst of her explanation, recognizing it as substantially her own version of responsible Mormon parenting as she had outlined it to him the week before. She understood the gospel principle fully; she just had been blinded to its applicability to her everyday challenges as a parent.

In the remainder of this chapter, I should like to share three gospel-derived, interrelated marital survival principles that may be labeled collectively *The Law of the Harvest.* They apply with equal force to temple marriages or to any other kind, but my concern here is with the potential eternal union. When these principles are observed, husband-wife relationships prosper; when they are ignored, relationships wither and die and, in that process, become toxic to the souls of the participants.

PRINCIPLE I: WATER, FEED, AND FERTILIZE

The first principle related to the Law of the Harvest is this: *Marital relationships, like all living things, require regular nourishment to thrive.* This point is vividly illustrated by a series of studies on the impact of pregnancy and childbirth on marital morale. One set of investigators tracked marital morale among a group of couples over the first five years of their marriage. They noted that among those who had no children over the five-year span, there was a slow but steady decline in the enthusiasm the couple had for the marriage. This effect had been observed in other studies and seems to be the normal result of the disillusionment that occurs when the often unrealistic expectations many couples bring with them to marriage collide with the complexities of actual marriage experience.

Couples who had a child during this initial five-year span of marriage also experienced this expected decline, but in addition, suffered a precipitous drop-off in marital morale during the pregnancy and the early infancy of the child. After the first few months of parenthood, the marital morale recovered in some degree, but it never regained the level of those who had no child over the same span of months.

Some of the couples had not one, but two children during the period of the study. These suffered the same loss of marital morale as others during the pregnancy and the early infancy of their first child and then a similar drop with the second child. The recovery from this second dip fell short of the level achieved by those with only one child (let alone the level maintained by those with none).

You can readily appreciate that this finding might be unnerving to someone like my wife and me who have had eight children. If the pattern found in this study held for all eight pregnancies and early infancies, our marital morale should have been doomed to end up in some emotional sub-basement.

The good news is that it doesn't have to be that way. Other studies have shown that some couples manage to inoculate themselves against the loss experienced by most couples in these circumstances. Those who manage to avoid the dip are likely to have three characteristics that set them apart from others.

First, they jointly planned and wanted the baby. Studies show that about half of all babies come as the result of failed contraception. Such babies can be cherished also, but the advantage, both for the child and for the marital relationship, is with the eagerly anticipated and warmly welcomed child.

Second, in these happier couples the husband is very much more likely to have been involved in the pregnancy, the delivery, and the care of the newborn. He is the type who informs himself about fetal development at each stage of the pregnancy and proudly exhibits sonograms to his friends; he is very likely to have attended Lamaze classes and coached his wife through the challenges of the labor and delivery processes; he is available to give the baby its first postpartum bath and is active in its care from that point forward.

Third, these couples do not get so wrapped up in the process of becoming parents that they forget to be marital partners; they plan and protect time to be alone with each other. It may not be possible to achieve this as easily or as often as before the baby complicated their lives, but they manage it regularly and reliably. These occasions are the pillars that support the roof of their marital morale structure. As any architect knows, supports do not need to be placed right next to each other to do the job, but if they are spaced too far apart, the roof will surely sag.

Of course, this principle not only applies to couples coping with becoming parents but is operational also at every other point in the marital relationship. If couples hope to maintain a vital, bountiful relationship, they need to understand that they must protect and nourish it on a regular basis. Part of this is refusing to let other important life tasks (the children, the job, demanding parents, or church assignments) crowd out the prime relationship. They structure their time and energy so that significant segments of their life are shared and so that the pillars of their relationship do not stand too far apart.

PRINCIPLE II: WEED, WEED, WEED

One of the disturbing features of gardens and of relationships is that if you only take thought to nourish the crop you may yet lose the harvest because of weeds. I know many a couple who spend a great deal of time together in shared activities but the result is toxic because the nature of the interaction is noxious. Three of the most common and destructive marital weeds I observe among those with temple marriages are these: 1) well-rationalized mismanagement of anger and disappointment; 2) well-intended but toxic and erosive criticism; and 3) unacknowledged, nonverbal "metamessages" that challenge or demean the partner.

1. *Mismanaged Anger and Disappointment.* It is not possible for any couple to live together for any extended period without each of the partners experiencing irritation and disappointment. But some styles for handling these natural feelings are particularly harmful, not only to the quality of the relationship, but to the individual spirits of the partners. In the classic case, one partner may acknowledge (almost with pride) that he or she has a "short fuse" or a "hot temper." Probably it has been shaped and legitimized by generations of forebearers who were fine people who also had hot tempers. From time to time, as irritations reach some critical point, there comes the characteristic explosion of unkind and often all but unforgivably hurtful words and actions. Afterward the person feels much relieved and in a mood to forget the whole thing. Perhaps, if the reaction of the spouse is extremely negative, there may be promises never to do it again. But, of course, the promise is not kept.

It would not be uncommon for the partner with this

destructive, self-indulgent addiction to be married to a spouse who is afflicted with the equal and opposite addiction, the "slow-burning, self-pitying, resentment-hoarding" that never lets go of a hurt and sours both the relationship and the character of the hoarder. Those who have experienced either or both of these styles can testify that they are weeds, indeed, and can choke out many a loving seed that might otherwise thrive.

2. *Well-Intended but Toxic Criticism.* A bright and worthy young doctor married an equally bright and worthy (and, judging by her wedding pictures, very beautiful) young woman in the temple. That night, the magical, long-awaited intimate moment came when, as he put it, he unwrapped the package to see just what he had bought. The first, loving, romantic, never-to-be-forgotten words out of his mouth were: "You know, honey, you could lose a few pounds."

It should be noted that this intense young physician gave high priority to physical fitness in his own life. His food intake was meticulously monitored as to both balance and amount. He ran six miles before breakfast every morning. He would doubtless have sunk like a rock in the Great Salt Lake. His comment was well-intended. Yet some readers, at least, will not be surprised to learn that despite an enormous amount of well-intended—and knowledgeable—guidance, effort, and supervision on his part, by the time I saw them in therapy eleven years later, far from having lost the original "few pounds," this woman had ballooned up to over 300 pounds. How could this have happened? Especially, how could it have happened given the remarkable good fortune of having a bona fide M.D. weight expert in her own home who was willing to invest any amount of energy or money to help!

If this seems perplexing to you, ask your spouse to explain the dynamics of it.

I do not want to leave the impression that this pattern of toxic but well-intended criticism is a characteristic peculiar

to virtuous LDS men. In fact, based on my clinical observation, I would wager that most of the world records in this
event are held by faithful, loving, competent, helpful LDS
women. The righteous desire of their hearts is to help their
foot-dragging patriarchs become the priesthood leaders in
their homes that they could and should be, but are not.
Often the results of their unflagging efforts are as impressive
as our young doctor's, and as disappointing and perplexing.

Studies have shown that the optimal diet for a happy
marriage provides a ratio of nine positives (nondemanding
touches, kind words, compliments, upbeat comments) for
one negative (criticisms, complaints, reminders, accusa-
tions, requests, demanding touches). Would you care to
guess the national average? Various studies put it at about
seven negatives for every three positives. My guess is that
this is about the average for temple marriages also, although
I know of no research on this population. In any case, most
would agree that there is room for improvement in the ratio
of positives to negatives in most "celestial-kingdom-bound"
relationships.

3. *Unacknowledged "Metamessages" that Challenge or Belittle
the Partner.* Students of human communication have pointed
out that every exchange of messages contains two parts: the
"message," which contains the manifest content of the communication, and the "metamessage," which is carried in the
way the message is presented—the tone of voice, the inflec-
tion, the body language—which *defines the relationship*
between the sender and receiver. A comfortable, symmetrical, straight-across exchange may indicate an egalitarian or
equal relationship. On the other hand, if the metamessage
is judgmental or arrogant, it communicates that the sender
feels the receiver is inferior, or if it is worshipful, that the
receiver is felt to be superior; if it is well-defended and sus-
picious, the receiver is defined as dangerous and untrust-
worthy, if open and loving, as safe and trusted.

Because metamessages are rarely put into words they are

hard to pin down. Frequently senders deny any intention of sending such messages and may not even acknowledge to themselves the feelings they reveal to the sensitive receivers. But never doubt that relationships thrive or waste away based on the impacts of these relationship-defining exchanges. Again, the findings of a long-term study of marital success and failure come to mind. In this case the investigators had newly married couples participate in a "hot debate" on some subject that they disagreed on. This debate was videotaped and the individuals were also monitored for blood pressure, pulse, and palm sweat. The exercise was repeated every year for five years in one study and nine in another. By the end of that time a certain number had already separated or divorced. The investigators were interested in seeing whether they could identify a "debate" pattern that predicted eventual failure. Surprisingly, the most damaging pattern was *not* the symmetrical hot debate, despite the yelling that sometimes occurred. The key to these couples' survival was that the *metamessage,* even in these relative free-for-alls, was "we are equals." The most damaging pattern was a vicious cycle that involved the wife trying to get the husband involved in the discussion and his stonewalling her. One can debate who was the more at fault, him for his stubborn refusal to cooperate or her for her dogged persistence and pursuit. The more relevant point is that the *metamessages* exchanged by these couples were, "We are competitors for control of this relationship." Independent of the content of the quarrel, the style was a power struggle. Relationships are often the losers in contests of will.

The same study also had another finding that was pertinent to our discussion. Couples were asked to fill out questionnaires before they did the "hot-debate" exercise. The single item that best predicted survival over the whole five- or nine-year course of the study was this: "Husband voluntarily and cheerfully participates in housework."

I routinely ask audiences of LDS couples why on earth this item should be so remarkably predictive. Is getting the housework done expeditiously *really* the key to marital survival? Of course the answer is that it is the relational message in the "voluntarily and cheerfully" part of the question that is the key. The metamessage from the husband to the wife is validating, loving, and egalitarian. One woman came up after the discussion to confide that although she had been reluctant to bring it up in front of all the other couples, for her, "voluntary and cheerful participation in housework" was foreplay.

I cannot sufficiently emphasize the point that we are not typically conscious of the messages we send. My children have pointed out to me a couple of truly embarrassing defects in my own metamessage repertoire. I have always prided myself on my tolerance of other people's opinions. "Let them believe how, where, or what they may" is my motto. I have often bragged that I have encouraged my children to think through issues on their own and that I invited calm and open discussions of any alternative views. As evidence, I have pointed to the 1992 U.S. presidential elections where various members of my family passionately endorsed and voted for each of the three major candidates. But not too many months ago, I was interrupted in the midst of such a boast by one of my children who noted that it wasn't like that at all. What really happened when one of them put forth an opinion at variance to my own, was that I rolled my eyes and sighed (as much as to say, "I can't believe that my own flesh and blood could come up with such an idiotic idea"). *Then,* I would assume the posture of the tolerant, sponsoring mentor of individual variations of opinion. My attempt to deny any such signal was shouted down by a chorus of affirmations by other family members. "Dad," they said, "your opinions on everything are transparent. Don't you know that when you were bishop nobody ever watched the sacrament meeting speaker? Everybody watched you to see how the speaker was doing."

Even more embarrassing was their further observation (they were on something of a roll at their dad's expense) that I walk ahead of everybody whenever we go out as a group—and sometimes even when I'm on a date with their mother. Ouch! What kind of a metamessage is that? So I'm trying to raise my consciousness on these matters and change my ways. But, I figure that if *I* who give lectures and write books on this stuff can be so unaware of my own ungracious relational messages, others must find it challenging also. Certainly it is my observation as a therapist and as a people-watcher outside of therapy that I am not alone in this.

PRINCIPLE III: PROTECT FROM PREDATORS

In the Savior's parable of the sower some of the good seed was plucked up by fowls and never survived to fulfill its promise. In this permissive and erotically supersaturated world, we lose a lot of temple marriages to predators. Temple covenants are restrictive, oppressively so, to some who observe all around them people of their own social class and standing enjoying the pleasures of the flesh with the approval of most of their associates. We live in a consumer-oriented culture, and many feel that the "Joneses" are having more fun than they are. Haven't we worked just as hard as they? Yet we are being cheated of many of the gratifications and rewards that others demand as their right.

Others, who would never let themselves be tempted by such obvious Sodom and Gomorrah stuff, are yet led carefully away by ignoring the safety rules that ought to protect one's marital commitment. In their efforts to do good, to comfort those that mourn, to cheer up the brokenhearted, they do not guard themselves from getting first emotionally and then physically involved with needy and appreciative people who happen not to be their spouses. I do not feel the need to belabor the point. If the promise of eternal marriage and exaltation is likened to a seed and a bird eats it, there won't be any rich celestial harvest, whatever the motivation of the bird.

IN CONCLUSION

When it comes to celestial marriage, it is not a matter solely of whether the marriage itself survives, but, as suggested by the title of this piece, whether the individual partners survive with their spiritual well-being intact. One of the hazards of making such lofty promises and indulging in such elevated hopes is that when it all turns sour, as it does in too many cases, the disappointment is as extravagant as the expectation had been. Sometimes Humpty-Dumpty can be put back together again, with or without the help of wise friends, sensitive priesthood leaders, or competent therapists. Sometimes it even happens that the loss of innocence is good for the relationship, in that each partner has learned through their painful experience the importance of principles they had too cavalierly overlooked.

Sometimes there is no resuscitation possible. The wounding is too great or one's partner has stubbornly turned away from the path that leads home. There is yet survival and even celestial promise for those who endure, faithful to the end. For some, a wiser, richer marriage with a worthy second partner. For some a lonelier journey, lighted by the faith that every modern prophet has taught that our God will withhold no blessing from any of his children that they would willingly receive if the circumstances of their lives permitted it.

For the grateful majority of us, the marriage survives our mistakes, and serves, if we will permit it, as a continuing University of Advanced Gospel Application. The principles we learned in Primary; but the day-to-day applications—ah, there's the continuing challenge.

PART III

---

*Three Pastoral Letters
on Christmas*

CHAPTER 9

Reflections on Christmas

For a change of pace, here are three pastoral letters on Christmas.

Every year Deseret Book puts out a little Christmas volume to celebrate the season. For the 1992 version, they invited me to submit something. At first I couldn't think of what to send; then I remembered that every month while I was bishop of the Cerritos Third Ward, I had written pastoral letters to the members. I pulled out the December letters for 1989, 1990, and 1991, and thought they might do. Deseret Book was kind enough to include them in the 1992 volume *The Magic of Christmas: A Collection of Stories, Poems, Essays, and Traditions by Favorite LDS Authors.* I include them here, hoping that others might enjoy them also.

SYMBOLS OF THE SEASON

I know that most of the symbols associated with the Christmas season have non-Christian origins, but for me, these pagan symbols are like all of us—subject to redemption. By their long and faithful association with the Savior's birth, they have acquired sanctified meanings that transcend their origins. I do not know or care what the original significance of the Christmas tree might have been. To me the evergreens of Christmas are tokens of the hope that life and fragrance and beauty can survive the hostile surrounds of winter. Christ is the true author of eternal life. Through him, we too can survive life's storms and freezes with dignity and vitality. Though planted in a sometimes hostile environment, we too can be evergreen.

To me the lights of Christmas are the tokens of the Light of the World, whose birth we celebrate. As the colored lights of the season brighten our lives and beautify our surroundings and guide us through the chill of night to the warmth of home, so the Savior's love and sacrifice bring hope and joy, and light the way to our eternal destination.

I have heard the custom of exchanging gifts at Christmas vilified as commercialism that detracts from the significance of the day, but to me, nothing better symbolizes the spirit of giving and of sacrifice that we celebrate that day. It reminds me of him who "gave his only begotten Son, that whosoever believeth in him should not perish, but have everlasting life" (John 3:16), and his promise that "If you keep my commandments and endure to the end you shall have eternal life, which gift is the greatest of all the gifts of God" (D&C 14:7).

I love the symbols of the Christmas season, all of them. They convey no pagan messages to my eye or ear. To me they shall ever speak—no, *carol*—the glad tidings of my Savior, and of the difference he has made in my life.

A CHILDREN'S HOLIDAY

Christmas is a children's holiday, and that is as it should be. It celebrates the coming of a baby, who when he had grown to be a man said, "Suffer the little children to come unto me, and forbid them not: for of such is the kingdom of God" (Mark 10:14). Christ's treatment of little children was truly remarkable. When he came to the Americas he also called for them to be gathered and brought to him, and he blessed them and gave them power to prophesy great and marvelous things to their parents. It is not recorded that he ever scolded a child or asked the parents of a crying baby to leave the congregation so that others might hear him more clearly. All of us know that even the best behaved of children have a naughty streak in them, but Jesus seems never to have addressed that part of them. Instead he was unfailingly appreciative of their innocence, commending it as a model for their parents' imitation. He was protective of them, declaring that if any would purposely offend one of these little ones, it were better that a millstone be hung around their necks and they be drowned in the deepest sea. To all of us who have sometimes felt less charitable toward our own or others' children, it gives food for thought.

What did the Savior see so clearly in children that we sometimes lose sight of? Perhaps he was less distracted by their misbehavior and more in touch with who they really were: angels come from the presence of God to test themselves against the often cruel challenges of earth life. Perhaps he remembered them as fellow members of the royal household of heaven, who not long since had walked and talked with him in the cool of his Father's and Mother's celestial gardens. Perhaps he foresaw and felt compassion for the pains and disappointments and mistakes that would all too soon rob them of their innocence. Perhaps he rejoiced in a divine awareness that his own sacrifice would open the door for each of them to find their way back home again. Whatever it was that he saw so plainly, and we so dimly, it persuaded him to bless and honor the children rather than correcting or chastising them.

As parents, it is, alas, our recurring duty to do both sets of things: to correct and chastise as well as to bless and honor our children. But at Christmastime it is somehow easier to bless than to correct, to honor than to chastise, to be more like him whose birth we celebrate. We rejoice in this unique Spirit of Christmas, which surely emanates from him. And while the Spirit is still upon us, it is almost possible to remember that we too, each of us, are also children in his eyes—worthy also of blessing and honor, despite our misbehaviors, because of who we are to him.

THE NOAH PERSPECTIVE

When we tell the Christmas story it is common to focus on the perspective of Mary or Joseph, of the shepherds or the wise men, of the people of Judea or those of the Americas. I should like to consider it from the viewpoint of another key participant: Noah. In the Gospel accounts of those events he is called the Angel Gabriel, but in life, as the Prophet Joseph told us, he was Noah of the Flood, Noah of the Ark.

There were doubtless many reasons why the Father of us all chose Gabriel for this particular mission rather than, say, Michael, who in life was Adam, or Raphael or one of the other heavenly messengers. It is not given to us to know any of those reasons. But I cannot help wondering if it had something to do with the parallels between the two assignments. In life, Noah's task was to warn the people to repent lest they be destroyed and to build a single ark to save the few who would listen. He faithfully performed that assignment. Was it not, then, fitting that among the faithful in the spirit world, he be the one chosen to warn the people anew and to announce the advent of the Eternal Ark, Christ Jesus, in whom alone the listener could find safety.

He was the messenger trusted to communicate to a tender young woman the news of her astonishing and unprecedented assignment. He was the comforter who assured Joseph that his intended was not only virtuous, but blessed above all women. I am confident that his was the voice that announced Christ's coming to the shepherds. In life he had been a faithful steward; in death he was given an extraordinary trust. I bear witness that all that he told men on those occasions is true. Christ was and is the Savior of mankind, just as Gabriel announced so many years ago. Noah's glorious postmortal privilege was unique, but it was also a type and shadow of the rewards and opportunities that God reserves for all who love and serve him in this life.

PART IV

The Most Meaningful Articles I Ever Had the Privilege of Producing

CHAPTER TEN

The Familial Relationships of Jesus

Peter certainly had the right of it when he acknowledged that we are a peculiar people. Just to cite one striking example, among what other people in the history of the world has it been considered standard operating procedure for someone (for anyone with a slip of authorization from his or her bishop) to phone an ordinary mortal and make an appointment to receive an open revelation from God? (Will eight o'clock Tuesday evening be all right?) The calling to serve as a patriarch in the Church must surely be unique in all the world. And although each of us with that responsibility must harbor, somewhere deeply buried in our imperfect souls, a primal fear that on some future day we may be called up before the Patriarchal Blessing Quality Control Board ("Broderick, what on earth could you have been thinking telling young George Anderson . . .")—still, I have a great testimony of the validity of this ordinance. For one thing, my own blessing, which I received at the tender age of nine, literally tells me everything that I will do in my life. One line in particular haunts and encourages me. I was promised that I would write literature that would bless. I think that's a gutsy thing to foresee in the life of a skinny, wiseacre, nine-year-old boy.

In this section I have included three articles that, I believe, may be a partial fulfillment of that assignment. The other two chapters I have seen bless the lives of others in a degree that is humbling and gratifying. But this chapter . . . this chapter I include here because it blesses me. It has been one of the tenderest gifts I have ever received from my Savior to be given the privilege of being the one chosen to pull together the snippets concerning his personal relationships in his family, which are scattered throughout the scriptures, into a single coherent account. I testify that I was guided through that process by the Spirit. When it was finished I wept. I wept at the personal familial pain that he bore, beyond the supreme vicarious suffering of Gethsemane. And I wept at the gift to me to be its chronicler.

My original assignment was to do a piece for the *Ensign* magazine on the Savior's teachings about the family. It was to be one of a series of articles in support of the Gospel Doctrine course of study that year, which was the New Testament. I took the assignment with some reluctance because although I love the scriptural account of the Lord's life, it was my impression that it was seriously lacking in any uplifting sermons on the family. There was his rather unkind treatment of his mother and brethren when they attempted to reach him while he was preaching; there was his telling the would-be disciple who wanted first to bury his father to let the dead (better translation, *the village*) bury the dead; there was his declaration that he had come not to bring peace but to "set a man at variance against his father, and the daughter against her mother, and the daughter in law against her mother in law. And [that] a man's foes shall be they of his own household" (Matthew 10:35–36). There were the tender and forgiving encounters with the three adulterous women; and there was the proclamation about there being no marriage or giving in marriage in heaven. I think I do not exaggerate when I say that this is not a promising set of proof texts for the article I am sure the *Ensign* wanted.

I called and talked to them about it. Perhaps, I suggested, they might want me to write about *Paul's* family doctrine. Although he has an antifamily reputation, actually I have found Paul to be extremely wise in his counsel. Wel-l-l-l . . . they already had several articles assigned for the second half of the year. Couldn't I do something with the Gospels? So I settled down with my yellow pad and the New Testament. Somehow, I got distracted from my mission and started culling out scattered references to the brethren of the Lord. John said they were unbelieving. In another place they taunted Jesus about not going up to Jerusalem during one of the annual feasts (knowing full well there was a price on his head). A pattern, a story began to emerge. It was poignant, it was real, it was personal. It was what I had to write about.

The *Ensign* accepted it. But as their letter of acceptance said, they had "heavily edited" it. Some of the deletions and rewording were, I thought, helpful, but most had the effect of reducing the drama, the feelings, and the story I had discovered. Much of the wonderful understanding that I had felt came from the Spirit had gotten diluted. I have no standing in the Church that gives me the right to receive inspiration for any but myself; however, since no one would mistake the present volume as scripture, I have provided here the whole of the article.

Finally, I should like in the introduction to the article and not as part of it, to indulge in a little further speculation that makes sense to me, but that goes beyond the data. It concerns the wedding at Cana. I have come to believe that this was indeed the wedding of Jesus' youngest sister. It was the custom for marriages to take place in the groom's father's home. The father was the "ruler of the feast." But it was, then as now, the parents of the bride who were in charge of the food and drink. Jesus had, I would assume, taken the duties of the senior male in the family once Joseph had died. It is conceivable to me that he had participated in the rearing of his youngest brothers and sisters. In this light, the miracle at Cana becomes not a trivial party favor to make his mother look good, but a final exercise of his surrogate paternal responsibilities toward his beloved youngest sister, a fulfillment and conclusion to his family responsibilities before turning to the full-time pursuit of his Messianic destiny. My testimony doesn't hang on that interpretation, but it is a scenario that rests easy on my spirit.

THE BROTHERS OF JESUS:
LOVING THE UNBELIEVING RELATIVE

Many of us have a father or mother, husband or wife, brother or sister, son or daughter, who rejects the gospel we hold so precious. Many compassionate and helpful sermons have been given on how best to handle this situation, but I have never heard one that attempted to examine how the Savior dealt with that problem in his own family.

Certainly the scriptural record is skimpy, and doubtless Jesus addressed many gracious acts and words to his unbelieving brothers that are not recorded in the surviving accounts of his earthly ministry. Nevertheless, we can learn much from the few incidents that have been preserved and from the final outcome of Jesus' labors with his family.

Mark 6:3 tells us that Jesus had four younger brothers and at least two sisters, the children of Mary and Joseph. The sisters' names have not been preserved, but the brothers were called James (in the Hebrew, *Jacob*), Joses (in the Hebrew, *Joseph*, after his father), Simon, and Judas or Juda also known as Jude (see also Matthew 13:55).

Although there is no scriptural evidence for it, tradition claims that when Mary's husband died, her eldest son, Jesus, took over Joseph's business and supported the family until his brothers and sisters were married or independent. Even if that were not true, by the time Jesus was thirty, evidently his mother was a widow, and as the oldest male in the family, Jesus was sought out when there were important family matters to consider, even after he had given up his carpenter tools and engaged full-time in his ministry (see Matthew 12:46–47).

They were a close family. After the marriage at Cana (because of Mary's and Jesus' roles at the feast, the wedding was most likely that of a close relative), Jesus invited the whole family to accompany him and the small group of his earliest disciples on his first recorded missionary journey to nearby Capernaum. Perhaps he hoped that by being exposed to his teachings and the miracles he performed, they would be converted and come to comprehend the true nature of their elder brother and his mission.

In many ways the first weeks of his ministry were full of glorious successes. Luke says of that first missionary journey, "And Jesus returned in the power of the Spirit into Galilee: and there went out a fame of him through all the region round about" (Luke 4:14). Yet, when he and his little group returned to Nazareth where he had been brought up, and he declared his Messiahship to his former friends and neighbors, the response was uniformly hostile. The congregation became so angry at his claims that they attempted to cast him off a cliff. He escaped, but it is not recorded that any brother's voice or hand was raised in his defense (see Luke 4:16–30). The sad truth is that, despite their exposure to his words and his works, "neither did his brethren believe in him" (John 7:5).

Months later, during a second missionary journey through Galilee, Jesus revisited Nazareth. Although he had established himself as a prophet and a healer whose name had become well known in the land, the Nazarenes' response was so derisive that he exclaimed, "A prophet is not without honour, but in his own country, and *among his own kin, and in his own house*" (Mark 6:4; emphasis added).

We can only imagine the degree of Jesus' pain at this rejection by those he loved. Perhaps we get some glimpse of it on one occasion when his mother and brothers interrupted a meeting at which he was teaching the gospel. We don't know the reason for the interruption, but his family may have wanted Jesus to attend to some family matter they felt was important.

"Then came to him his mother and his brethren, and could not come at him for the press.

"And it was told him by certain which said, Thy mother and thy brethren stand without, desiring to see thee.

"And he answered and said unto them, My mother and my brethren are these which hear the word of God, and do it" (Luke 8:19–21).

Some have considered Jesus' words to be harsh. But the Savior knew what his family did not yet fully realize—that the bonds of faith and covenant are stronger than the bonds of blood, and that his role as eldest son in the family, which they honored, was of little significance compared to his role as Savior and Redeemer.

He was, in fact, saying to them no more than what Abinadi had said almost two hundred years earlier. Speaking of the Christ who should come, Abinadi taught:

"When his soul has been made an offering for sin he shall see his seed. And now what say ye? And who shall be his seed?

"Behold I say unto you, that whosoever has heard the words of the prophets, . . . all those who have hearkened unto their words, and believed that the Lord would redeem his people, and have looked forward to that day for a remission of their sins, I say unto you, that these are his seed" (Mosiah 15:10–11).

The Savior's disappointment and pain at the faithlessness of his earthly brothers were much more poignantly revealed at Calvary. There, in the final minutes of his agony on the cross he looked down at his distraught mother, weeping together with a little cluster of brave disciples who risked their own lives to be there during his final ordeal. She had four other sons, yet none were present to comfort her. None were disciples, committed to love God and one another and to follow the way he had taught. Only his beloved John was there. With what mixed feelings he must have groaned his last will and testament: "He saith unto his mother, Woman, behold thy son! Then saith he to the disciple, Behold thy mother! And from that hour that disciple took her unto his own home (John 19:26–27).

After this, knowing that all things were now accomplished, Jesus said, "It is finished: and he bowed his head, and gave up the ghost" (John 19:28, 30).

But that is not the end of the story. Before considering what we might learn from the Savior's experience, we need to follow the course of his brothers' lives after the Crucifixion.

Paul relates that after the risen Christ had appeared to Peter, then to the other Apostles, and then to five hundred of the worthy brethren, Jesus appeared also to his brother James (see 1 Corinthians 15:5–7).

The details of that reunion are not available to us, but the results are. James and his brothers responded as did Saul of Tarsus and Alma the Younger and the four sons of Mosiah. The brothers not only repented, but they became committed servants of Christ—their eldest brother—and eventually powerful leaders in the early Church.

Immediately following the ascension of Christ, the Apostles returned to Jerusalem to the home of John Mark's mother: "When they were come in, they went up into an upper room, where abode both Peter, and James, and John, and Andrew, Philip, and Thomas, Bartholomew, and Matthew, James the son of Alphaeus, and Simon Zelotes, and Judas the brother of James."

Then Luke makes this revealing observation: "These all continued with one accord in prayer and supplication, with the women, and Mary the mother of Jesus, and with his brethren" (Acts 1:13–14).

At last, the brothers of the Lord had taken upon themselves his name and become, in very truth, members of his family!

James quickly rose to a position of leadership. Indeed, Paul implies that James became an Apostle. Three years after his conversion, about A.D. 38, Paul traveled to Jerusalem to meet with a few Church leaders. He wrote of that experience: "I went up to Jerusalem to see Peter, and abode with him fifteen days.

"But other of the apostles saw I none, save James the Lord's brother" (Galatians 1:18–19).

At another time during a period of intense persecution, Herod killed James the brother of John and imprisoned Peter (see Acts 12:1–4). When an angel came and freed the chief Apostle, he fled immediately to the home of Mary, the mother of John Mark, where some of the disciples were gathered together praying. After describing his escape, Peter instructed them to "go shew these things unto James, and to the brethren" (Acts 12:7–17).

A few years later, Paul and Barnabas attended a council at Jerusalem concerning Jewish requirements for gentile Christians. Only Peter seems to have had a more influential position at the meeting than James, and James was the one who proposed the final accepted solution (see Acts 15:6–31).

Paul, in referring to that event, wrote of "James, Cephas [i.e., Peter], and John, who seemed to be pillars" (Galatians 2:9). Quite possibly, James the brother of the Lord filled the position in the Church leadership left vacant by the death of that other James who had served with Peter and John.

Whatever his exact position in the early Church government, we treasure James's general epistle to the Church. For it was this James who wrote—one must believe out of his own painful and glorious experience with his resurrected brother—"If any of you lack wisdom, let him ask of God, that giveth to all men liberally, and upbraideth not; and it shall be given him" (James 1:5).

In that epistle, he identifies himself not as the brother of the Lord, but as "James, a servant of God and of the Lord Jesus Christ" (James 1:1). Though others referred to him, Jude, Simon, and Joses as "the brethren of the Lord," James himself was loath to assert his special kinship, preferring to be known as a servant of Christ.

In a similar vein, another of the four brothers opens his epistle with "Jude, the servant of Jesus Christ, and brother of James" (Jude 1:1). We know little about Jude except what we learn from his epistle. Most impressively, Jude demonstrates a keen perception of his elder brother as the past and future Lord—the Lord who brought Israel out of Egypt and who destroyed Sodom and Gomorrah, and the Lord who will come in the last days to execute judgment upon all (see Jude 1:5, 7, 14–15).

From his denunciation of certain kinds of apostasy, we also know that his letter was one of the later epistles in the New Testament. In his lifetime, Jude stood firm with Peter and Paul in fighting the rising tide of heresy that threatened to destroy the Church.

All four brothers, family members who had once looked at Jesus as their elder brother only, were able to accept him as the Lord and the Son of God. What great joy there must have been in heaven, and especially for the Savior, over these four brothers, each of whom repented.

It is true that the Savior's family was unique. No other family has had to come to terms with its close relative turning out to be the Redeemer of mankind. But in another sense, every converted person who deeply loves his or her unbelieving spouse or relative suffers as Jesus suffered over his faithless brothers. And, as did Jesus of Nazareth, every disciple can love truly and well, with hope and patience.

We must never lose sight of the eternal realities—the worth of each soul, the inviolability of each soul's agency, and the universality of the plan of salvation. Above all, we must never give up.

It is well to remember that those of whom it was once written "Neither did his brethren believe in him" ended by designating themselves servants "of God and of the Lord Jesus Christ." So it may be for our Jameses and our Judes, our Sauls and our Almas, and all of their female counterparts. In a personal, intimate way, Jesus himself suffered so that he is able to succor them that also suffer (see Hebrews 2:18; Alma 7:12).

CHAPTER ELEVEN

What Justification Can There Be for Innocent Children Being Born into Abusive Families?

I can take no credit for the healing concepts that are presented in these final two chapters. They came from God. My heart does swell with joy and gratitude that I have been privileged to be a vehicle for their dissemination. Wherever I travel in the Church, whatever my assigned topic, there are always those who come up afterward to let me know that their lives have been given richer meaning by these insights into the broader definition of what it is to be "a savior on Mount Zion."

Although the concept is thoroughly rooted in the unique understanding that Mormons have of premortal life, it may be surprising to learn that it travels well. It has worked miracles of healing among Protestants and Catholics and Jews who somehow manage to find a way to incorporate it into their own sense of God's dealings with his children (Jews, for example, have a long tradition of the "suffering servant"). It even translates well into the secular world, given that it requires a more acceptable label. In my secular textbooks I honor those "transitional characters" who refuse to pass on the destructive, toxic parenting they received. Even this humanistic version can be observed to have healing power. It gives meaning to the sacrifice and recognition to the courage of those who have committed their lives to purifying a lineage.

The first of these pieces was a response in the "I Have a Question" section of the *Ensign* in August of 1986. The second, a more broadly based discussion of "The Uses of Adversity," was given at BYU Women's Conference in 1987 (in the Marriott Center in front of seven jillion women, by far the largest live audience I ever faced). I include them both here, confident that in the writing of these two pieces, at least, the promise in my patriarchal blessing was fulfilled.

THE QUESTION OF ABUSED CHILDREN

Q: *So many children are abused, offended, and abandoned. If little children are precious to God, what justification can there be for permitting some to be born into such circumstances?*

A: As children of God, we have been given the great gift of choice. We may choose to help, or we may choose to hurt. Unfortunately, as the Lord explained to Moses, the iniquities of one generation are often visited upon the heads of following generations (see Exodus 20:5). Anyone can see the truth of that saying by looking at many families in the world today. Often, troubled families seem to pass on their pain and darkness—virtually intact—to their children and grandchildren. The victim of one generation becomes the victimizer of the next.

On the other hand, the Lord told the prophet Ezekiel: "What mean ye, that ye use this proverb concerning the land of Israel, saying, The fathers have eaten sour grapes, and the children's teeth are set on edge?

"As I live, saith the Lord God, ye shall not have occasion any more to use this proverb in Israel.

"Behold, all souls are mine; as the soul of the father, so also the soul of the son is mine: the soul that sinneth, it shall die" (Ezekiel 18:2–4).

This scripture suggests that children need not merely replicate the sins of their fathers, but that each generation is held accountable for its own choices.

Indeed, my experience in various Church callings and in my profession as a family therapist has convinced me that God actively intervenes in some destructive lineages, assigning a valiant spirit to break the chain of destructiveness in such families. Although these children may suffer innocently as victims of violence, neglect, and exploitation, through the grace of God some find the strength to "metabolize" the poison within themselves, refusing to pass it on to future generations. Before them were generations of destructive pain; after them the line flows clear and pure. Their children and children's children will call them blessed.

In suffering innocently that others might not suffer, such persons, in some degree, become as "saviors on Mount Zion" by helping to bring salvation to a lineage.

I have had the privilege of knowing many such individuals—people whose backgrounds are full of incredible pain and humiliation. I think of a young woman who was repeatedly abused sexually by her father. When at last she gained the courage to tell her mother, the girl was angrily beaten and rejected by her.

These experiences made the girl bitter and self-doubting. Yet, despite all odds, she has made peace with God and found a trustworthy husband with whom she is raising a righteous family. Moreover, she has dedicated her energies to helping other women with similar backgrounds eliminate the poison from their own lineages.

I think of a young man whose mother died when he was twelve and whose father responded to that loss by locking his son in his room, then drinking and entertaining women in the house. When he would come to let the boy out, he would beat him senseless, sometimes breaking bones and causing concussions.

As might be expected, the young man grew up full of confusion, self-hate, and resentment. Yet the Lord did not leave him so, but provided friends and opportunities for growth. Today, through a series of spiritually healing miracles, this young man is preparing for a temple marriage to a good woman. Together they are committed to bringing children up in righteousness and gentleness and love.

In a former era, the Lord sent a flood to destroy unworthy lineages. In this generation, it is my faith that he has sent numerous choice individuals to help purify them.

In the days of Jeremiah, the Lord used some of the same language he would later use in speaking to Ezekiel: "In those days they shall say no more, The fathers have eaten a sour grape, and the children's teeth are set on edge.

"But every one shall die for his own iniquity: every man that eateth the sour grape, his teeth shall be set on edge" (Jeremiah 31:29–30).

Then he went on to say of this new, covenant generation, "I will put my law in their inward parts, and write it in their hearts; and will be their God, and they shall be my people" (Jeremiah 31:33).

Most of us, I believe, are acquainted with one or more of these valiant, struggling spirits. In the latter stages of their progress, they are easy to recognize and appreciate. But sometimes in the early stages they are suffering so much from their terrible wounds that it takes a mature degree of spiritual sensitivity to see past the bitterness and pain to discern the purity of spirit within. It is our duty and our privilege to befriend such individuals and to provide whatever assistance and support we can in helping them to achieve their high destiny.

Others of us may be, ourselves, the suffering messengers of light. Let us be true to our divine commission, forgoing bitterness and following in our Savior's footsteps.

CHAPTER TWELVE

The Uses of Adversity

While I was serving as a stake president, the event occurred that I want to use as the keynote to my remarks. I was sitting on the stand at a combined meeting of the stake Primary board and stake Young Women's board where they were jointly inducting from the Primary into the Young Women's organization the eleven-year-old girls who that year had made the big step. They had a lovely program. It was one of those fantastic, beautiful presentations—based on the *Wizard of Oz*, or a take-off on the *Wizard of Oz*, where Dorothy, an eleven-year-old girl, was coming down the yellow brick road together with the tin woodman, the cowardly lion, and the scarecrow. They were singing altered lyrics about the gospel. And Oz, which was one wall of the cultural hall, looked very much like the Los Angeles Temple. They really took off down that road. There were no weeds on that road; there were no munchkins; there were no misplaced tiles; there was no wicked witch of the west. That was one antiseptic yellow brick road, and it was very, very clear that once they got to Oz, they had it made. It was all sewed up.

Following that beautiful presentation with all the snappy tunes and skipping and so on, came a sister who I swear was sent over from Hollywood central casting. (I do not believe she was in my stake; I never saw her before in my life.) She looked as if she had come right off the cover of a fashion magazine—every hair in place—with a photogenic returned missionary husband who looked like he came out of central casting and two or three, or heaven knows how many, photogenic children, all of whom came out of central casting or Kleenex ads or whatever. She enthused over her temple marriage and how wonderful life was with her charming husband and her perfect children and that the young women too could look like her and have a husband like him and children like them if they would stick to the yellow brick road and live in Oz. It was a lovely, sort of tear-jerking, event.

After the event was nearly over, the stake Primary president, who was conducting, made a grave strategic error. She turned to me and, pro forma, said, "President Broderick, is there anything you would like to add to this lovely evening?"

I said, "Yes, there is," and I don't think she has ever forgiven me. What I said was this, "Girls, this has been a beautiful program. I commend the gospel with all of its auxiliaries and the temple to you, but I do not want you to believe for one minute that if you keep all the commandments and live as close to the Lord as you can and do everything right and fight off the entire priests quorum one by one and wait chastely for your missionary to return and pay your tithing and attend your meetings, accept calls from the bishop, and have a temple marriage, I do not want you to believe that bad things will not happen to you. And when that happens, I do not want you to say that God was not true. Or, to say, 'They promised me in Primary, they promised me when I was a Mia Maid, they promised me from the pulpit that if I were very, very good, I would be blessed. But the boy I want doesn't know I exist, or the missionary I've waited for and kept chaste so we both could go to the temple turned out to be a flake,' or far worse things than any of the above. Sad things—children who are sick or developmentally handicapped, husbands who are not faithful, illnesses that can cripple, or violence, betrayals, hurts, deaths, losses—when those things happen, do not say God is not keeping his promises to me. The gospel of Jesus Christ is not insurance against pain. It is resource in event of pain, and when that pain comes (and it will come because we came here on earth to have pain among other things), when it comes, rejoice that you have resource to deal with your pain."

Now, I do not want to suggest for a moment, nor do I believe, that God visits us with all that pain. I think that may occur in individual cases, but I think we fought a war in heaven for the privilege of coming to a place that was unjust. That was the idea of coming to earth—that it was unjust, that there would be pain and grief and sorrow. As Eve so eloquently said, it is better that we should suffer. Now, her perspective may not be shared by all. But, I am persuaded that she had rare insight, more than her husband, into the necessity of pain, although none of us welcome it.

I remember one time thinking such thoughts, such grand thoughts, and realizing that I dealt as a therapist with many people who suffered far, far more pain than I ever suffered and feeling guilty at having been spared some of the pain that my friends had experienced. Shortly after this, I developed a toothache. I'm a great chicken—I hate pain at all times. An apocryphal story was told of my mother who, as she took me to kindergarten, told the teacher I was very sensitive and, if I didn't behave, to hit the child next to me. Although that's not a true story, it truly represents my sentiments. I'll learn from others, although I don't want pain myself. So when I had this toothache, I thought, here is a golden opportunity to embrace this existential experience and to join in this pain—open myself to this pain and experience it. I told myself I'm just going to sit in this pain and take it into myself and grow from it. That lasted forty-five minutes, at which time I called my dentist, "I want some pain medicine." The forty-five minutes it took between the time I took the medicine and the time the pain went away was the hardest part because I showed no moral stature; all I wanted was to get rid of that pain.

So I do not want you to think that I believe anything good about pain. I hate pain. I hate injustice. I hate loss. I hate all the things we all hate. None of us love those things. Nor, as I say, do I think God takes pleasure in the pain that comes to us. But, we came to a world where we are not protected from those things. I want to talk to you not in behalf of pain—heaven forbid—nor do I think that all pain is for the best. I'm certain that's not true. I'm certain pain destroys and embitters far more often than it ennobles. I'm sure injustice is destructive of good things in the world far more often than people rise above it. I'm certain that in this unjust awful world, there are far more victims that do not profit from their experience than those who do. So I do not want you to think I'm saying that pain is good for you. Pain is terrible.

I want to talk rather about when pain unbidden and unwanted and unjustly comes—to you or to those that you love or to these eleven-year-old girls as they get along in their lives. I want to discuss how to encounter that pain in such a way that it does not destroy you, how to find profit in that awful and unrewarding experience. I want to share with you some stories, mostly not my own, although I'm in all of them, but the pain is mainly someone else's. Some of the pain is my own. All of it is real, and all of it taught me. What I want is not to lecture to you or to sermonize you, but to share with you some lessons I have learned through pain, my own and others', that are valuable to me and, in the end, to share with you what I think I have learned from those incremental experiences.

The first two stories were extraordinarily instructive to me. They both came through opportunities I had as a stake president to give blessings. Often the Lord has taught me through blessings; as I've had my hands on someone's head, he's taught me things I did not know and sometimes didn't want to know. The first one was a case of a sister whom I'd known for years and who, in my judgment, had made some very poor life choices. She had married a handsome, charming young man who initially wasn't a member of the Church but joined the Church for her. She waited a year to marry him and then went to the temple. It was the last time he ever went to the temple. I knew he was a flake from the beginning. Out of my wisdom, it didn't surprise me that he soon returned to many of his prechurch habits—most of the transgressions in the book that you can think of and some that I might not have.

There was great pain for this woman. A good, good woman, she kept in the Church; she kept in the kingdom; she suffered enormous pain because her husband went back to gambling and drinking and other things that were unhappy and unwholesome. But, the greater pain came when her children, having these two models before them, began to follow him. He would say things like, "Well, you can go to church with your mother and sit through three hours of you know what, or you can come to the racetrack with me, and we'll have good stuff to eat and drink and have a great time." It was a tough choice, and very often the children chose to go with him. They gradually seemed to adopt his lifestyle, values, and attitude toward the Church and toward sacred things. Although she never wavered from her own faith and faithfulness and her commitment to her Heavenly Father, her family was slipping away from her.

As she asked me for a blessing to sustain her in what to do with this awful situation in which she found herself, my thoughts were, "Didn't you ask for this? You married a guy who really didn't have any depth to him and raised your kids too permissively. You should have fought harder to keep them in church rather than letting them run off to racetracks." I had all those judgments in my head. I laid my hands on her head, and the Lord told her of his love and his tender concern for her. He acknowledged that he had given her (and that she had volunteered for) a far, far harder task than he would like. (And, as he put in my mind, a harder task than I had had. I have eight good kids, the last of whom just went to the temple. All would have been good if they had been orphans.) She, however, had signed up for hard children, for children who had rebellious spirits but who were valuable; for a hard husband who had a rebellious spirit but who was valuable. The Lord alluded to events in her life that I hadn't known about, but which she confirmed afterwards: twice Heavenly Father had given her the choice between life and death, whether to come home and be relieved of her responsibilities, which weren't going very well, or whether to stay to see if she could work them through. Twice on death's bed she had sent the messenger away and gone back to that hard task. She stayed with it.

I repented. I realized I was in the presence of one of the Lord's great noble spirits, who had chosen not a safe place behind the lines pushing out the ordnance to the people in the front lines as I was doing, but somebody who chose to live out in the trenches where the Lord's work was being done, where there was risk, where you could be hurt, where you could lose, where you could be destroyed by your love. That's the way she had chosen to labor. Then I thought, "I am unworthy to lay my hands on her head; if our sexes were reversed, she should have had her hands on mine."

Now she is doing well; one of her sons finally went on a mission. He had a bishop who took hold of him and shook him and got him to go. He went to one of those missions where people line up to be baptized when you get off the plane. He had a wonderful mission; they all but made an icon of him. He had miracles under his hands. He came back hotter than a firecracker for missions. He wouldn't leave alone his younger brother, who was planning on playing football in college instead of going on a mission, until he also went on a mission. The younger boy looked up to his brother; nobody could have turned that second kid around except his older brother. The younger went on a harder mission. He happened to have a language skill that he developed, and he turned out to be the best one at the language. He caught fire; he had spiritual experiences, and he came back red hot.

Those two boys started working with their sisters, who are harder cases; they haven't come all the way around yet. One of them looks better. One of them married a nonmember, and her husband did a terrible thing—he met the missionaries and joined the Church and started putting pressure on his wife to become active. She said, "I married you because you were out of the Church." I don't know—even Dad may repent, who knows? You know, she may yet win them all.

I know that she risked her life for service. In a blessing the Lord said to her, "When you're in my employ, the wages are from me, not from those you serve."

In the second case I had a woman who came to me who was an incest victim—the victim of a terrible family. She was abused physically. Her mother was neurotic and stayed in bed all the time to get her daughter to do all the work, including taking care of the husband's needs when he was drunk. The daughter had been abused in about every way there was to be abused—psychologically, physically, sexually. Besides that she had to do all the housework.

She was not a member of the Church at that time, although this happens to members of the Church also. In high school she met a young man who was a Latter-day Saint and who started taking her to church with him. Eventually they married. He was gentle and kind and patient because she didn't come with very many positive attitudes toward men, marital intimacy, or many other things. But he was long-suffering and patient and loved her. They raised some boys.

Despite this, she had recurring bouts of depression and very negative feelings about herself because she had been taught by the people most important in her early life what a rotten person she was. It was hard for her to overcome that self-image. I worked with her to try to build her self-image. One day she said to me, "You're a stake president." She wasn't in my stake, but she said, "You're a stake president; you explain to me the justice of it." She said, "I go to church, and I can hardly stand it. When I see little girls being hugged and kissed and taken to church and appropriately loved by their fathers and mothers, I just have to get up and leave. I say, 'Heavenly Father, what was so terrible about me that, when I was that age, I didn't get any of that? What did that little girl do in the premortal existence that I didn't do so she is loved, so she is safe? Her daddy gives her priesthood blessings when she's sick. Her mother loves her and supports her and teaches her. What did I do?' Can you tell me that God is just if he sends that little girl to that family and me to my family?" She said, "It's a good thing I had boys. I don't think I could have stood to raise girls and have their father love them because I'm so envious."

I would not have known how to answer her in my own capacity because that is manifestly unjust. Where here or in eternity is the justice in an innocent child's suffering in that way? But the Lord inspired me to tell her, and I believe with all my heart that it applies to many in the kingdom, that she was a valiant, Christlike spirit who volunteered (with, I told her, perhaps too much spiritual pride) to come to earth and suffer innocently to purify a lineage. She had volunteered to absorb the poisoning of sin, anger, anguish, and violence, to take it into herself and not to pass it on; to purify a lineage so that downstream from her it ran pure and clean, full of love and the Spirit of the Lord and self-worth. I believed truly that her calling was to be a savior on Mount Zion: that is, to be Savior-like, like the Savior to suffer innocently that others might not suffer. She voluntarily took such a task with the promise she would not be left alone and abandoned, but he would send one to take her by the hand and be her companion out into the light. I viewed that woman in a different way also, again realizing I was in the presence of one of the great ones and unworthy to have my hands on her head.

I think we do not understand the nature of ourselves. I think we do not understand who we are. Some people call the temple ordinances the "mysteries" of the kingdom. When I went to the temple, I thought I was going to learn which star was Kolob, where the Ten Tribes were, and other such information. But those aren't the mysteries of the kingdom; the mysteries of the kingdom are who we are, and who God is, and what our relationship to him is. Those are the mysteries of the kingdom. You can tell somebody in plain English, but they still don't know in their hearts who they really are.

I was in a foreign country giving a workshop for others in my profession. The workshop was over, and I was just exhausted. My plane was to leave at 7:30 P.M. back to the States, and it was now 4:00 P.M. I was right across the street from the airport in a motel. I thought, "This is nap time. I am going, in the middle of the day with the sun out, to take a nap." So I called the desk and said, "I want to be awakened at 6:00, not 6:00 in the morning but 6:00 in the evening; I'm taking a nap." I put down the receiver, undressed, and curled into bed and thought how deliciously wicked it was to be sleeping in the middle of the day. I had just snuggled down when the telephone rang. It was the mission president, who also was a General Authority whom I had never met, but who had read in the paper that I was there. He had a problem with one of his sister missionaries. Although he'd been working with her, she had a ticket to go home on the same flight I was on. He'd labored with her and given her blessings. She'd only been out six weeks, but she was going home and nothing he was able to say changed her mind. The mission president said, "She said she had your text in college, and I told her you were here. I asked her if she would see you, and she said she would." He said, "You're it."

I protested, "It's your job; it's not my job. You're a General Authority—I'm just a stake president and out of my territory at that."

He said to me, "We'll send the car for you."

This sister and I sat down together. She had her purse clutched and her ticket prominently displayed on it. She looked at me a bit defiantly, and I said, "The president tells me you're headed for home."

She answered, "Yes, and you can't talk me out of it either."

I said, "Why?"

She told me why.

It was an awful story. She did grow up in a Mormon family in Idaho—a farm family, a rural, poor family. She had been sexually abused, not just by her father, but by all her male relatives. She was terribly abused. Incidentally, I want to tell those of you who teach girls this, she had tried to tell a couple of times, and people wouldn't believe her. When she was ten years old, they had a lesson in Sunday School on honoring your father and mother. After class was over, she said to her teacher, "But, what if your father or your mother wants to do something that isn't right?"

The teacher said, "Oh, my dear, that would never happen. Your father and your mother would never want anything that wasn't right for you."

Finally, when she was fourteen, her Mia Maid teacher believed her and convinced the bishop it was so. The bishop took her out of that home into his own home where she finished her high school years; he sent her to college, and then she went on a mission. Her father's "patriarchal blessing" when she left his home was this, "Well, aren't we fine folk now? Gonna go live with the bishop and all those holy joes over on the other side of town. Well, let me just tell you something, girl, and don't you never forget it. They can't make a silk purse out of a sow's ear." That's what she decided on her mission. She decided she didn't belong there with all those silk purses. She was having sexual feelings for the missionaries because when you're only four or five when you first get exposed to regular sex, it isn't easy. You don't have the adult's or the teenager's sense of proportion and sense of reality and sense of the world to put it into proportion. So here were all these attractive young men, and she'd never had the opportunity to develop in her life the kinds of protections in her heart and in her mind that other people in more blessed and protected circumstances have. She was having feelings that she believed were unworthy and told herself, "My daddy was right. You can take a girl out of a family and send her to college, you can send her on a mission, but you can't change what she is—a sow's ear."

So she was going home to throw herself away because she didn't belong out here pretending to be someone she wasn't. I said to her, "Before you came on your mission, you went to the temple, didn't you? You were anointed to become a queen, weren't you, a princess in your Heavenly Father's house? That's no way to treat a princess. There may be—I can't imagine it—but there may be some justification in their backgrounds for the way those men treated you when you were young. I don't know; I can't imagine any. But, I'm confident of this, the Lord will not easily forgive you if you treat his daughter that way. You're going to throw her away, a princess of our Heavenly Father? Then what are you going to say to him when he says, 'How have you handled the stewardship that I gave you of this glorious personage who lived with me, who is my daughter, who is a royal personage of dignity and of honor? I sent her down to the earth, and how have you brought her back to me?'" She with the eloquence of her age and circumstances started to cry, but she stayed.

I saw her in Provo two or three years later when I was there speaking. She asked if I remembered her, and I did, which was a miracle in its own right because I forget my own children's names; I can't get them all straight. I remembered her and her name and said, "How are you doing?" She answered, "I'm growing just as fast as I can. I thought you'd want to know." She understood who she was. I told her that I felt her stewardship was to get that daughter of our Heavenly Father home, home to Heavenly Father, home where she belonged. That's the mystery of the kingdom, that's the mystery of godliness—that we are our Father's children.

Now I'm going to tell you three other stories. One of them concerns a sister I used to home teach years ago. She was something. President Benson was president of the Quorum of the Twelve and he was the one who sent out the schedules specifying when stakes would hold their conferences. For several years in a row we always had our stake conference on Mother's Day. It was nice because we saved money on carnations, but this lady was outraged. She couldn't see why it always had to be our stake on Mother's Day. She wanted the carnations and the respect for women. So she finally wrote a stern letter to President Benson calling him to repentance for not observing the importance of motherhood. She said the priesthood leaders talked a good fight, but where were they when it really counted on Mother's Day? And he changed the date of our stake conference. So you get some feel for this woman—a good woman, but not shy.

Anyway, I was her home teacher and her stake president. She was also one of those sisters who felt that if you just have a cold, it's all right to have your husband give you a blessing, but if it's anything more serious, you need at least the bishop. Stake presidents are better. If there's a General

Authority in the area, that's the best. She wanted real sparks—none of this homegrown stuff.

They had two or three girls, and she'd had troubles with her deliveries, which were caesarean. Her doctor told her that she had nearly died the last time. He said, "Your uterus is so thin that when I was working there, I could see my hand through it. It is not going to sustain another pregnancy. If you want to die, get pregnant again. Is that very clear? Will you let me take it out?" She said, "No." He said, "It's no good except to kill you." She said, "Don't take it." So he said, "All right, but I want you to know that if you have another pregnancy, you're dead."

Well, that lasted about four years. I accused her of having gone to see *Saturday's Warrior* one time too many. She decided they had a little boy up there waiting to come to their family. Her husband said, "Oh, no, you don't. You think you're going to get pregnant and leave me to raise those girls without you. No way; I'm not going to do that. The doctor told you, and that's sensible, and that's it."

"But I just feel there's still one up there for us."

"No way. We are not going to take any risks with your life. I'm not up to raising three daughters alone. I'm sorry; 'no' is the answer."

"Well, when President Broderick comes, let's have him give me a blessing."

Well, he got to me first, of course, and I couldn't have agreed with him more. I didn't want that on my hands. That's what we have doctors for. So I was not very moved by this woman's ambition to have one more child and said, "Now look, Sister so-and-so, you can't do this." But this lady is not an easy person to say no to. So her husband and I laid our hands on her head, and I heard myself telling this lady, Sure, go right ahead and have a baby. No problem. You'll have no problem in the pregnancy; it'll be just fine. You'll have a fine big boy, nurse him, and everything will just be terrific. I could not believe I was saying it. Her husband was looking at me in horror. I left immediately.

But it happened just like the blessing said. It was just one of those stories where the Lord gives you the answer. She got pregnant. The doctor shook his head, but when the baby was delivered, it was fine. The uterus was fine; the baby was terrific. One little hitch—only it wasn't a little hitch; it was a big hitch. In the hospital somehow she had contracted a blood disease, Haverman's disease. I'd never heard of it before, and I've not heard of it since, but it's vividly etched in my memory. She broke out in spots all over. They're very irritable, like having the skin off your hand or off your back. She had at one point two hundred spots all over her body. She couldn't lie down or sit down or be comfortable anywhere, and they looked awful. It looked as though she ought to wear a veil to cover these big, red, size-of-a-fifty-cent-piece blotches all over her body. There was a medication she could take to relieve the symptoms. Although it doesn't cure the disease, it does make the symptoms go away and allows you to live and function normally. But she wouldn't be able to nurse her baby if she took it.

"You promised in the blessing," she said, "that I could nurse this baby."

I said, "It was a throw-away line. What are you talking about?"

She said, "You promised, the Lord promised I could nurse this baby. I can't nurse him and take medication so you have to do something about this."

I said, "Look, get a bottle. Your husband can get up in the middle of the night. It'll be terrific. Take the medication; you're home free—the baby's fine. Rejoice, you've got a beautiful boy."

She would not have any of that. She wanted another blessing to take away this disease so she could nurse her baby. I wished I were not her home teacher, not her stake president. But I put my hands on her head, and I heard myself telling her that her disease would go away and she would be able to nurse her baby. Then I left for New York— not just because of that. I had a meeting in New York, but I was glad not to be there hour by hour to see how it worked out.

I gave the blessing on a Sunday evening. Wednesday at two o'clock in the morning, I got a telephone call while I was in a deep sleep. I was president of this national organization and worrying about the next night when I was to give my presidential address. It was hard to sleep, but I was doing my best. The call woke me, and she said, "You promised me these spots would go away, but they're worse. I visited the doctor today, and he says they're worse. Nothing's going well. You promised. I've done everything I know to do. I've been on the telephone all day to people that I might have offended, even in my childhood. 'Please, please, if there's anything I've done to offend you, please forgive me.' I'm trying to think of anything I've ever done in my life and to set it right. But my spots haven't gone away. Why?"

"I don't have any idea why," I said.

She retorted, "Well, don't you think you ought to have an idea. You gave me that blessing."

I felt terrible. I did something I've never done before or since—I stayed up the rest of the night, what there was of it, praying. I said, "Lord, this woman's faith hangs on the blessing she received at my hands. I felt your Spirit at the time. If I was wrong, don't penalize her. Cover me." (And I started thinking of the people I should be calling.)

But she didn't call again, and I thought maybe it's all right. I got home Saturday night late, flying all day from New York, exhausted from the trip. I walked into the house, and there was a note that said, "No matter what time you arrive, call sister so-and-so." I didn't dare not do it, so I phoned her. She said, "You get on over here." Is that any way to talk to a stake president?

It was two o'clock in the morning, but I went over. She was bitter and empty. She said, "I want you to know that I have no faith left. I felt the Spirit of the Lord, the same Spirit when you gave me that blessing, that I've felt in sacrament meetings, in testimony meetings, when I read the scriptures, and in prayer. I felt that same Spirit, and here's my testimony." She raised her hands, which were covered with spots. "Well," she said, "what have you got to say?"

"Nothing."

"Don't you think you owe me an explanation?"

I said, "I have no explanation. I prayed all night. I don't have any idea why. I feel awful that I've been the instrument of your loss of faith. I cannot think of a worse thing that could have happened, that I could have spent my priesthood on, than to destroy your faith."

"Don't you think you owe me an explanation?"

"I tell you I have no explanation."

"You and the Lord—don't you think you owe me an explanation?"

"I'm not giving you any more blessings."

She said, "I think you owe me that, don't you?"

I never did anything with less grace in my life than when I laid my hands on her head. The Lord spoke to her, not of her disease and not of nursing babies, but of his love for her—that she was his daughter, that he cared for her, that he had died for her. He said that he would have died if she had been the only one. He would have suffered at Calvary for her sins, if hers had been the only ones. He didn't say one word about healing her.

The next day was fast Sunday. She came to church although she had said she never would again. With the spots she looked awful. It was not easy; she was not an overly proud woman, but it was not easy for her to appear in public looking as she did. She got up in testimony meeting, and her spots were worse than ever. She told the story and at the end she said, "I do not know why I have these spots, why my breasts have dried, but I do know this." And she bore a powerful witness of the Savior's love for her. That afternoon the spots went away and the milk came in, but not until she understood the mysteries of the kingdom, which don't have much to do with spots or milk or even with blessings, but have a lot to do with who we are and who our Father is, who our Savior is, and the relationship among the three of us.

I'm going to tell just two more stories. My mother, I trust, did not have a typical Mormon woman's life. She married three times, but she got better at it as she went along. I've been grateful to her that she didn't stop until she got a good man. He wasn't a member of the Church when she married him, but he did join the Church and eventually became a bishop—a very good man. I'm sealed to him, and I love him. I wear his ring. He wanted me to have it because in his family when somebody died, people quarreled over the tea cups. He wanted me before he died to have the ring so no one would quarrel over it, and I could have it. I wear it with love.

He died, in some ways, in a bad way, a hard way. He was a strong man—a man who'd been a sickly youth, but he'd done some of the Charles Atlas exercises. I used to love to hear him tell about how eventually he'd turned the table on the bullies. I was one who always ran away from bullies, walked to the other side of the street and went home the other way, but I loved to hear his stories about how he'd finally gotten strong enough to take them on and beat them at their own game. I had a lot of vicarious satisfaction from his stories.

But at the end his lungs filled up with fiber so he had only five percent of his lungs to breathe with. With only five percent of the oxygen that he needed to metabolize his food, he just got weaker and weaker. His bones showed everywhere on his body. This big, beefy, all-solid-muscle man got to the point where all of his muscle had been eaten alive. I could easily carry him in my arms, although I'm not a strong man physically. He became petulant and childish because he could hardly breathe. He was constantly asphyxiated. He could hardly eat or go to the bathroom because he didn't have the oxygen to close his mouth that long. What a strain to see this strong, good man waste away.

A week before he died I asked him for a father's blessing. He could reach over only one hand because he couldn't find a position where he could breathe and get both hands together. He gave me a blessing; I'd never had one in my life before. With one hand, he gave me a father's blessing, which I treasure. Then I asked him—and it was more talking than he had done for a long time in one space—I asked, "Vic, what have you learned from this six months of wasting away?"

He said, "Patience; I was never patient. The Lord has taught me patience. I wanted to die six months ago, and he left me. I've had to wait upon him. You know those stories I used to tell?"

"Yes, the ones I liked so well."

"Son, those aren't good stories; they're full of revenge. They're not loving stories. I repent of them."

That man did not waste those six months. How many of us would have gotten bitter at God? "Why don't you take me? I've done everything; all I want to do is come home." That man spent those months being refined. I know he's presiding today over his family. We've done genealogy for his forebears and sent them up to him to work on in the spirit world. I know he presides over them today, and I know he's a better president of his familial branch in the spirit world than he was a bishop, and he was a good bishop. But, I know he was refined by his pain, by his adversity. He needed to go through that suffering. He could have been embittered; he could have been destroyed. His faith could have soured and left him, but he chose to learn from his pain. I do not want you to think that it was the pain that was good. It was the man that was good and that made the pain work for him, as indeed our Savior did.

Last Easter a friend, after having brought two boys, then four and two, into the world, had a baby daughter. While she was in the hospital, her husband wanted to come to see the baby, but he had those little children at home. So his home teacher was kind enough to say, "Hey, bring the kids over. We've got a bunch of kids at our house. Bring the two kids over; my wife'll watch them." (That's not quite what King Benjamin said about service, but it's one step off.) "You go and see your baby."

So he did. While he was in the hospital seeing his new baby, his two-year-old got away from that woman's care and drowned in the pool. Through CPR she was able to bring him back to his heart beating and his lungs working but never to real functioning. For two months he lay in a hospital bed, breathing, with his heart beating on machines that helped. His little knees somehow (I don't understand the mechanics of this) bent backwards. His feet bent backwards. I don't know why. In the rigidity of his coma he became deformed. He had been a perfectly whole, wonderful child, but now it was hard for me to go visit him. I would go and sit beside him, looking at his mother who was rubbing him and singing to him. It was hard.

The ward fasted every Sunday for a month for that child. The members kept a twenty-four-hour vigil so that there'd be somebody he knew there when their faith made him whole. He was blessed by the stake patriarch, by the stake president, by a visiting General Authority who was kind enough to add that additional duty to his busy schedule. In all those blessings the mother took hope. I will not say that she was promised flatly, but she took hope by what was said, that the child would live, that she would raise him in this life, and that he would perform many gracious acts and achievements. She would not even tolerate anyone's raising the possibility that he would not get better because she felt that everyone's faith had to be whole and focused.

I never saw so many people at the hospital—dozens of people kept vigil, fasted, and prayed for this child. After two months it became clear the child was wasting away and was not going to get better. His mother was the last to finally acknowledge what everyone else had come to see—he was not going to live. It was costing, I forget how many, thousands of dollars a day. So they finally decided to do the gracious thing and let him return to his Father. It was the hardest thing they ever did. They prayed, fasted, consulted with priesthood leaders, and finally, finally, decided the only thing to do was to pull the tubes. His mother said, "I can't stand it. I don't want to kill that little boy again. How many times is he going to die?"

So his grandmother went and held him in her arms when they pulled the tubes, but he didn't die. He lived another two weeks. I cannot express to you how spiritually exhausted everybody was when he finally died. The family had spent days and nights for weeks with him. Everybody had scarcely slept in two and a half months. Just a week before that child died, the newborn got a temperature of 105 and was taken to the hospital and diagnosed with spinal meningitis. It was a misdiagnosis, but they put the baby in the room just right down from the other baby.

Her husband said, "Honey, let me go bless the baby."

She said, "You get your priesthood hands off my baby." She didn't want God to take that baby too. She said, "God's got all the babies he wants. Why does he want my baby? God doesn't need him on a mission—don't tell me that." People are not always helpful with the things they say. "God needs him worse than I need him—don't tell me that. He's got billions of babies, and I only have one; I have one two-year-old. Don't tell me he has a mission that can't wait fifty or sixty years more on the other side. There's lots of work for him here. We'll keep him busy."

At the graveside the grandmother gave the opening prayer, and the grandfather dedicated the grave. In a somewhat unusual choice, both the boy's parents spoke. Can you imagine that? What they said was this: "We trust our faith will never again be tried as it has on this occasion. The things we have faith in have come down to a short list, but that list is immovable. We do not have faith that God must do what we entreat him to do." Earlier she had cried out to God, "I asked for a fish, and I got a serpent. I asked for a loaf, and I got a rock. Is that what the scriptures promise?"

But after it was all over, at her little son's graveside, she was able to say, "I am content that God be God. I will not try to instruct him on his duties or on his obligations toward me or toward any of his children. I know he lives and loves us, that he is God. He's not unmindful of us. We do not suffer out of his view. He does not inflict pain upon us, but he sustains us in our pain. I am his daughter; my son is also his son; we belong to him, and we are safe with him. I used to think we were safe from grief and pain here because of our faith. I know now that is not true, but we are safe in his love. We are protected in the most ultimate sense of all—we have a safe home forever. That is my witness."

And that is my witness to you, that God lives, and he does not live less though you have injustice and adversity and pain and unkindness and violence and betrayal. God is in his heaven. We chose to come to an unjust world and suffer. But God is God, and he loves us. His son died for us. There is for each of us, because of who we are and who he is and who we are together, hope. There is hope. The uses of adversity are whatever use we put them to—for you and for me, for the parents of the little boy, for the lady with Haverman's disease, and for the incest victims, for my dad, for all of us—the uses of adversity are the uses we put them to. May they hone us and purify us and teach us and not destroy us, because of who we are and who God is and what our relationship to him is, is my fervent prayer.

SOURCES

Chapter One, "My Parents Married on a Dare," is to be published in *Marriage and Family Review,* forthcoming. Used by permission.

Chapter Two, "The Core of My Faith," was first published in *A Thoughtful Faith: Essays on Belief by Mormon Scholars,* Philip L. Barlow, editor; Centerville, Utah: Canon Press, 1986. Used by permission.

Chapter Three, "Midlife Report," by Dr. Carlfred B. Broderick. First published in the *Ensign* magazine © The Church of Jesus Christ of Latter-day Saints (July 1979). Used by permission.

Chapter Four, "Summing It Up (Or, Why Let Somebody Else Write Your Obituary?)" is original to this book.

Chapter Five, "But What If Your Husband Is a Jerk?" was originally published in *This People* magazine, Spring 1995. Used by permission.

Chapter Six, "Marital Danger Zones," was originally published in *This People* magazine, Summer 1992. Used by permission.

Chapter Seven, "How Come Good People Can Have Bad Marriages?" by Dr. Carlfred B. Broderick. First published in the *Ensign* magazine © The Church of Jesus Christ of Latter-day Saints (July 1983). Used by permission.

Chapter Eight, "Surviving (Eternal) Marriage," was

originally published in *Eternal Companions*, edited by Douglas E. Brinley and Daniel K Judd, Bookcraft 1995. Copyright © 1995 by Bookcraft, Inc. Used by permission.

Chapter Nine, "Reflections on Christmas," was originally published in *The Magic of Christmas*, Deseret Book, 1992. Copyright © 1992 by Deseret Book Company. Used by permission.

Chapter Ten, "The Brothers of Jesus: Loving the Unbelieving Relative," by Dr. Carlfred B. Broderick. First published in the *Ensign* magazine © The Church of Jesus Christ of Latter-day Saints (March 1986). Used by permission.

Chapter Eleven, "What Justification Can There Be for Innocent Children Being Born into Abusive Families?" by Dr. Carlfred B. Broderick was first published in the "I Have a Question" section of the *Ensign* magazine © The Church of Jesus Christ of Latter-day Saints (August 1986). Used by permission.

Chapter Twelve, "The Uses of Adversity," was originally published in *As Women of Faith*, edited by Mary E. Stovall and Carol Cornwall Madsen, Deseret Book, 1989. Copyright © 1989 by Deseret Book Company. Used by permission.

INDEX

145